WEDDINGS AWAY

Weddings Away

The New Destination Wedding and
Getaway Wedding Celebrations Guide

Sharon Naylor

CITADEL PRESS
Kensington Publishing Corp.
www.kensingtonbooks.com

CITADEL PRESS BOOKS are published by

Kensington Publishing Corp.
119 West 40th Street
New York, NY 10018

Copyright © 2018 Sharon Naylor

All Kensington titles, imprints, and distributed lines are available at special quantity discounts for bulk purchases for sales promotions, premiums, fund-raising, educational, or institutional use. Special book excerpts or customized printings can also be created to fit specific needs. For details, write or phone the office of the Kensington sales manager: Kensington Publishing Corp., 119 West 40th Street, New York, NY 10018, attn: Sales Department; phone 1-800-221-2647.

CITADEL PRESS and the Citadel logo are Reg. U.S. Pat. & TM Off.

First trade paperback printing: February 2018

10 9 8 7 6 5 4 3 2 1

Printed in the United States of America

Library of Congress Cataloging-in-Publication data is available.

ISBN-13: 978-0-8065-3849-5
ISBN-10: 0-8065-3849-X

First electronic edition: February 2018

ISBN-13: 978-0-8065-3850-1
ISBN-10: 0-8065-3850-3

I dedicate this book to my husband, Joe,
the most amazing partner on every getaway
and at every destination.

And to my mother, Joanne,
who started me off on my love of travel
with the most wonderful vacations imaginable
in pre-Internet planning days.
The ocean loved you back.

Contents

Introduction

YOU'RE NOT ABOUT to plan a destination wedding. You're about to plan the best destination anyone you know (including you!) has ever seen, one that brings a level of heart and your relationship's personality to your getaway wedding…every day and every detail of it. We're about to slap away any doubts or trepidation you may have about planning a destination wedding, with lots of insider tips to help your planning process go smoothly, and your wedding weekend or week fabulous from start to finish. (And it might actually never be finished, since your friends and family in attendance will talk about your wedding for years upon years, and the memories from your ceremony and celebrations will live on with you forever. So we're going to make this good.)

You've seen dreamy destination weddings featured on your favorite wedding blogs, Instagrams and websites, in your favorite bridal magazines, and on those splashy reality show wedding specials. You've seen celebrity destination wedding images, and you may have attended several truly breathtaking destination weddings yourself. You know what you like. And even more, you know what you want to feel at your wedding. That's a big thing I want you to think about right up front, before we even get started. It's all about how you and your guests feel at your wedding, and at every event surrounding it. Of course, you want everyone to feel happy for you, excited about the food and entertainment, having the time of their life (as you have yours). Think, in addition, about how you can plan a wedding that makes your loved ones feel indulged, a bit spoiled from all of the VIP treatment, embraced, appreciated, and carefree. One of the best compliments I ever heard from destination wedding guests is that the wedding made them *feel* "younger," full of energy, without a care in the world, connected at last with friends and family they haven't seen in so long. They're free to shake their shyness, shake it on the dance floor, dive into the dessert bar, and have a few extra signature cocktails, the ones you planned and named so well. Real life is gone. They're here with you now, and—you want this to happen!— as happy for themselves as they are for the two of you. This, they will say, is the Best. Wedding. Ever. For how they felt as well as what they saw the whole time.

So that's our first big goal.

Our second big goal is for you to feel great during the planning process. And let me reveal the big secret right now: it's feeling like you've got this, not that it has you. Insider information and organization gives you that. I'm going to share with you some tricks to help you master the mechanics of your wedding planning without a worry, so that you can spend more time focusing on the beautiful parts, the elegance, the exotic touches you'd like to add to your wedding, your creativity, your vision, your wishes. The far more fun stuff. The gorgeous details you've been dreaming about (and pinning!) for a long time.

Our third big goal—and all three of these big goals are pretty much tied for top priority—is planning a destination wedding that is you. One that reflects your style and your great love, your story and your dreams.

First, we'll get the basics in line, and then we'll get creating. You'll see throughout the book little boxed features adding sprinkles of extra tips. Ones that I wanted to jump off the page at you. You'll find the following categories of tips:

- *Planning Smarts:* From-the-field smarts will give you an advantage in the planning.
- *Budget Tips:* These tips will save you money all the way through, from little savings to bigtime savings.

- *Destination Wedding Etiquette Tips:* You will want to keep these unexpected etiquette rules in mind, to help you avoid unforeseen etiquette mistakes that can wreck your wedding before you get to it.
- *Don't Forget:* From important things to pack to important questions to ask and rules to know, we lined up a stellar collection of reminders that can save the day.
- *Thinking About Your Guests:* These reminders are little and big things you can do for your guests' comfort and enjoyment at your getaway location.

Notice I said, "your getaway location." That's because this book includes planning details and tips on pre-wedding getaways, like a bachelorette trip instead of a bachelorette party, a Girls' Getaway that lets you celebrate with your ladies before your wedding trip. The guys are included, too, with Guys' Getaway ideas and tips to help (yes, maybe encourage!) them to skip the traditional bachelor party of debauchery and instead go someplace excellent, like on a ski trip, or to see a professional football game in a stadium across the country (and of course, you and your ladies can do those things as well! Or you can all go together, if that's your preference. The co-ed getaway trip gives you excellent quality time with long-time, long-distance friends. But we'll get to that later.)

Ready to get into it? You're already there. And I'm excited to join you in planning your dream destination wedding.

Part One

Pre-Planning Your Destination Wedding

This is where you'll set the foundation of your destination wedding, making all the big decisions like when, where, who to invite, who to hire, and other essential details from which all of your destination wedding ideas will spring. Take your time in this section, because these are some pretty important moves to make, ones that—once set—aren't easy to change, and that may demolish your wedding budget if you do have to change them. Deposits can be lost, relationships can be strained, and stress can skyrocket. Which can happen all the way through the process if you rush and make mistakes. So I'll start with some first essential tips:

1. *Be organized*. Super-organized. Especially when you're planning a destination wedding, a lot of your communications will be via e-mail and
phone, so keep those communications and your notes in one place so that
you can find them easily. Decide on an organizational system right now.
Will it be an online spreadsheet, a planning app, an old-school ledger, or
binder? What you don't want is little pieces of paper scattered everywhere,
making it impossible to find that note you made about a venue you have
in mind, or a deposit you made, a question you need to answer, or a person you need to contact. You're at the start of this thing now, and you
have no idea how much information you'll need to collect and be able to
retrieve. So expect a lot of details to keep track of, and start at minute

Planning Details

Lisa Lendino Plociniak, floral designer and artist at A Touch of Elegance Events, and stylist for celebrity weddings, shares some of her top tips for destination wedding floral design:

Best Flowers to Use in Hot and Humid Conditions

1. Orchids of all varieties—phalaenopsis, cymbidium, dendrobium—are most popular
2. Heliconia
3. Ginger
4. Mini calla lilies
5. Birds of paradise
6. Lilies
7. Tropical greens

These flowers are good because they have a waxy thicker texture that tends to hold more moisture than softer petal blooms like roses or peonies—the softer petal blooms do not work well in extreme heat

one with the most failsafe record-keeping plan you can possibly make. Because if just one important paper gets lost, it could cost you.

2. *Be open to your experts' suggestions.* Yes, you have a vision for your day, but excellent wedding vendors know from experience all of the little, surprise things that can potentially wreck your wedding. For instance, if your floral designer says that a particular kind of flower wilts very quickly in your chosen location's heat and humidity level, listen to that advice. It would be a terrible shame to have your wedding flowers wilted and half-dead before your guests even arrive. Keep an open mind as you keep your hand and heart on the ideas you bring to the table for best effect and your wedding's success.

because they wilt in warmer temperatures because they do not hold moisture as much. Granted please take into consideration all fresh flowers should always be handled with care in warmer climates and kept hydrated—because no matter what they can all have heat stress.

5 Tips When Planning Décor for Your Destination Wedding

1. *Choose flowers local and available to the island.* Anytime you import anything to a tropical island the taxes and fees associated may be just as expensive as the flower itself if not more.
2. *Remember that less is more when doing a destination wedding.* You are paying for the destination itself. As far as flowers I would consider bouquets, boutonnieres, and simple centerpieces and nothing too over the top—you are paying for the amazing view and the resort—which are already beautiful.
3. *Use the island as your ceremony backdrop.* Mother Nature has so much beauty—capitalize on it.
4. *Choose something unique from the particular country you are in as part of your décor.* Choose Mexican pottery at a Mexican destination or Venetian glass if you are in Italy.
5. *Consider family-style dinners.* Let your food become your décor.

3. *Step away from your wedding.* Close your laptop, get off of Pinterest, and take breaks from the planning to keep your balance and perspective. Make fun plans with your partner, friends, and family, go for a run, take a barre class, center yourself. Dissolving into your wedding at the expense of the rest of your life just builds up stress and leads to poor decision making, relationship strain, and budget disasters. You'll be a better designer of your destination wedding if you're coming from a rested, fulfilled place, not a panicky, obsessed place.

So that's three foundational tips to get you started, and you'll notice that they all play into your thinking and stress levels. Important stuff there. Mind them all, and your mind will be better equipped to plan your dream destination wedding.

1

Deciding on Your Destination Wedding Style

CHOOSING YOUR DESTINATION wedding style is a lot like shopping for your wedding dress. You may think you know exactly what you want, but just to be sure, "try on" a few different styles. You may just discover something else that feels really, really perfect for you. You didn't walk in thinking that would be The One, but once you've stepped into it, it transforms you. That original style you had in mind now pales in comparison. Or, you might "try on" a few different styles, stepping out of them even more convinced that your original choice was The One. You're completely confident in your selection, by giving the others some consideration.

First, Formality

Before we step into destination wedding styles tied to locations, let's first tackle your formality selection. How formal of a wedding do you want?

Keep in mind that a wedding set in an informal location such as at a beach or in a rustic barn can have many formal elements like chandeliers and fine linens, and that you can easily wear a formal dress at either of these types of locations. We're back to how you want your wedding to feel: formal with upscale elegance or laid-back. So answer these questions:

• Which elements of a wedding do you consider to be formal? (Table settings, floral arrangements, food service style like plated dinners on fine china, etc.) _____

_____

_____

• Which elements of a wedding do you consider to be informal? (Natural setting, menu options, drink styles, guest dress code, etc.) _____

_____

_____

Now, circle the ones that match the feeling you want for your wedding, and you'll show yourself a more fine-tuned vision of your wedding's formality.

Of course, you can always have your wedding team create details made of both formal and informal wedding elements, seamlessly planned and coordinated for your one-of-a-kind wedding that captures your love of classic wedding details

Planning Smarts

Yes, I am encouraging you to hire a wedding planner. Their fee is worth it for their expert input, years of experience in your style and scope of wedding, and the fairy godparent feel of having a pro save the day for you so many times!

but still sets a comfortable feel at your ceremony and celebration. Wedding planners and vendors are excellent at blending formality styles in ways that tie the entire event together without the kind of two-separate-weddings feel that can be the effect of working without expert visionaries.

Your Priority Lists

Now let's get into your priority lists, in which you each choose the top elements of your wedding that mean the most to you, that you want the most, and that will get the majority of your wedding budget so that you can do it up right. Here's what a sample priority list looks like:

Sara's Priority List

1. Venue
2. Wedding dress
3. Menu
4. Entertainment
5. Flowers

Sara's fiancé has a list that looks like this:

John's Priority List

1. Venue
2. Menu
3. Bar
4. Entertainment
5. Photography

Sara and John are on the same page with their venue, menu, and entertainment, so those are their shared top priorities. They then know to put their other top picks higher in their budget and planning effort.

Now, Sara and John will also ask themselves what they care least about, what they could potentially not include or spend money on. For them, it might be wedding programs and transportation (not needed, since their wedding takes place at a resort and they'll walk to their ceremony from their hotel rooms). You'll make your own low priority list as well, to help clear the decks at this early stage and give you more of an idea of how your budget will work. (Plus, it feels good to put some things in the Done pile, by virtue of not having to do them at all!)

You'll find Priority List worksheets at the back of this book for your use.

Destination Wedding Styles

Island

I'm sure you can picture it: your wedding processional leading you toes-in-the-sand to where your guests are seated in pretty white chairs set on a beach, with the azure blue ocean stretching to the horizon and a blue, cloudless sky above. Tropical flowers are everywhere, including tucked behind your ear, and a steel drum performer pounds out the notes of your islandy wedding march. The sun is warm on your shoulders, an ocean breeze makes the palm fronds dance above you, and colorful tropical drinks flow at your reception. That's one image.

Think also about a candlelit ceremony in the stone ruins of a sugar mill, with formally set, lantern-lit tables soon inviting guests to a lobster dinner with champagne aplenty as the sun sets dazzlingly over the ocean. Torches light the way to and from your unforgettable celebration.

Also in island wedding style is the island cruise wedding. You and your guests board a luxury yacht for a scenic sail around the islands at sunset, with your delectable island-inspired menu and drinks delighting your guests as your captain points out celebrity mansions set on the island cliffs. When you disembark, your guests are surprised to arrive at a bonfire on the beach, with your champagne and dessert buffet awaiting them.

Don't limit your vision to just beach-setting island weddings. There are plenty of sensational restaurants set on those cliffs as well, for superb service, gourmet menus, and picturesque scenery. And estate homes, which populate many of the world's best islands, open for renting for weddings and group stays. You get celebrity-style treatment by the owners' own personal butlers and staff, and when an estate home is linked to a nearby resort, you and your guests gain access to all of the amenities of the resort. It's a stellar destination wedding experience in VIP style.

Vineyard

Your wedding stage is set in the vineyard itself, with your ceremony taking place in a clearing among the arbors, and your tented reception treating guests to the wonderful, earthy feel of this setting. Strings of lights or a tent set off your celebration space, and wine and champagne are served with terrific food pairings for a spectacular experience your guests will love.

Or your wedding might take place inside the vineyard's architecturally gorgeous building, decorated to perfection with candles, fine linens, florals, and vineyard-perfect vines and greenery, again capturing that earthy feel with an upscale blend. At night, large lights in the distance provide an evening view of the vineyard land, and music rings out across the fields in celebration of your marriage.

Overseas City

Imagine a British castle reserved for your wedding, with guests staying in the castle for the weekend, transported to a royal wedding dream come true. The stone castle elicits childhood dreams of being a princess, and the history of the castle itself becomes part of your wedding's story. Fine-mannered servers treat your guests like dukes and duchesses, and an orchestra fit for a queen serenades your group with movie-style romance.

Think about a sun-washed island in Greece, with boats bobbing in the water and your wedding processional moving through the streets to your onlookers' joy (and your own). Take a walk through the cobblestone roads in an Italian village, perhaps at the same church where your ancestors married, and your al fresco celebration presenting guests with platter after platter of authentic Italian fare, fine wine, music sung in Italian, and pastries unlike the versions you've had at home. The lyrical sounds of another culture's language enriches your group's immersion into your wedding adventure, as does a weekend filled with shopping and excursions.

Overseas weddings can be formal or informal: city-set, country-set, or beach-set. While every wedding is filled with color, scents, and sounds, an overseas wedding seems to glow with so much more of these effects. Searching the world for

Think About Your Guests

When your destination wedding's style brings guests to a unique venue, they may get an extra bonus: one of their bucket list items crossed off! Thanks to you. They might never have actually booked a trip on their own to this wonderful place you've chosen.

the perfect exotic or overseas setting, with the help of your planner, can turn up a heart-fluttering unique venue for your wedding, a place that no one in your group has ever seen before, making this getaway wedding a dream vacation for all.

Domestic City

A city wedding evokes images of a modern loft with floor-to-ceiling glass walls overlooking the lights of the cityscape all around. Or a historic grand hotel ballroom decorated in splendor with five-star accoutrements and life-changing cuisine. A city wedding weekend can include outings to the theater with group-discount tickets, all the better if it's a surprise outing, as well as walks down legendary streets, stops at touristy spots, famous eateries, and fashion-forward shopping for all.

Imagine also a rooftop wedding, again with the jaw-dropping cityscape views, elegant décor, and the finest menu and drinks imaginable.

Cruise

Cruise weddings can be aboard large ships, with multiple wedding groups aboard and access to pools, water slides, shows, and buffets on board, as well as exotic port of call excursions adding extra adventure to your wedding experience.

You get multiple dining establishments, formal dinner nights, dancing, spa treatments, and shopping on board and wherever your ship may pull in. Or they might be aboard luxury private yachts decorated to your liking for your private wedding of five hours, or for an extended stay in staterooms for your lucky guests. These smaller boats might cruise waterways the bigger ships can't access, sail past skylines and landmarks, and be catered by the ship's own chef and staff.

Think about seasonal cruises, such as leaf-peeping fall cruises along a northern coast with spectacular views. Or an Alaskan cruise delivering you to a natural world of wonder, and again a bucket list destination for many of your guests, thanks to you. At any destination, you will get both onboard and excursion adventures and indulgences, and plenty of time for your guests to work their own itineraries into the mix.

National Park

Imagine your wedding held inside a national park, with mountains, colorful rock cliffs, cacti, and spectacular views all around you. If your chosen national park doesn't allow tented weddings within its confines, you'll find fine hotels and restaurants all around the perimeter, affording you sensational views and a ballroom feel at the same time. Those establishments know how to make the most of their phenomenal settings, and they know best the sunset times, so you may find outdoor tented weddings available on their grounds for your big sky wedding feel, minus the wildlife that may be present in the park.

This style of wedding is based in grandeur and love of nature, a sense of awe at the planet's creation, gratitude that places like this still exist in the world, and the unique pedigree of marrying there. Your guests will feel the same, and there's that bucket list thing again.

Garden

Speaking of magic, garden weddings are magical by nature, in that they are surrounded by the beauty of nature, an open-air step into a world of wonderment. Florals and greenery take the spotlight here, draped from trees and bursting forth from the ground, with some gardens' shrubbery art and waterfalls also adding to the mystique, and birds and butterflies visiting the wedding as if illustrated into the movie-worthy scene. Outdoor cocktail parties serve gourmet, garden-fresh fare, and the reception may be tented in fine formality or held in the nearby building for architectural wonder as well. Formal or informal, a garden wedding captures artistry of nature as well as the artistry of your floral designer and event planner.

Lake

I'm seeing lake-style weddings picking up in popularity, given the number of fine lakeside restaurants, resorts, houses to rent, and lakeside open-air spaces that can be booked for events. Even those childhood camps you may have loved are opening their off-season doors to weddings, and when the couple camped as kids, it can be tremendous fun to bring their loved ones into that beloved camp scene for a festive wedding and fun wedding weekend events. The camp lodge can be decorated in setting-matching style, or done formally with garlands of roses and greenery, gardenias, and orchids for upscale flair. Speaking of upscale flair, camp-type foods like short ribs and burgers can be prepared upscale-style with gourmet toppings and Kobe beef, artisan breads, and culinary treats like seviche to tie into the lakeside seafood feel.

Some wedding groups even lodge their guests in the cabins for an authentic experience, adding to their itineraries events like boating, hiking, horseback riding, and competitions like they enjoyed during their camp-going years. It's a style of wedding ideal for sharing stories of carefree childhood days, which beckons guests to share their own memories around the campfire while making s'mores. And beer is available out in the open, not just in the camp counselors' cabins.

A camp wedding or woodland wedding opens up some excellent décor and DIY opportunities for your wedding as well. Think of the words that remind you of camp—carefree, fun, adventurous, etc.—and apply them to this wedding style.

Resort

A fabulous resort welcomes your wedding to its manicured grounds, likely with a sensational view, fine dining, and a wedding package that can give you the presidential suite for free. If you buy out the resort for a big wedding, it'll be just your people lounging by the pool and filling the restaurants for mini parties left and right. Choose your style of wedding, from formal ballroom to a cookout on their lawn, and the resort's team will make it happen.

Planning Smarts

Always think about what the rest of your wedding weekend can entail when choosing a wedding style. Certain styles naturally pair up with certain activities like a winery wedding's natural flow into wine-tasting tours and balloon rides, or a resort wedding's group kayaking lesson. These wedding weekend activities have a feel of their own, which works together with your wedding's feel.

You may get that beach wedding you desire, with your reception held in the resort's ballroom for formal touches blended with informal or themed wedding décor, and your wedding weekend events can take place at the resort or via a venture off the grounds to other area attractions. For instance, a wedding at an amusement park's resort lets you and your guests spend a day going on rides and sharing in the excitement of their displays.

Winter Destination

Picture a pristine, fresh snowfall blanketing the ground and dusting the trees for as far as you can see in a wooded or mountainous setting that just takes your breath away. Picture a wood beam ceiling in the ski lodge, with guests sipping cognac and brandy by an oversized, roaring fireplace. Warmth all around. Your wedding takes on a snowy theme, with lots of white and crystals connoting icicles formed just for your big day, a sea of flowers, and lots of warm, spiked drinks for your guests. Imagine the excitement of your favorite ski excursions, your passion for skiing and snowboarding shared with your guests. Perhaps even your wedding signs written on snowboards at your wedding celebration.

Imagine arriving at your wedding in a horse-drawn sleigh for a movie-inspired grand entrance, and your guests primed for a destination wedding that's so unlike all of the tropical ones they've attended in the past. Your wedding reflects who you are as a couple, your great love for the winter season, and upscale design elements with a winter touch. Add in the indulgences of a great winter resort, includ-

Budget Tip

If your chosen style is woodland, ski resorts can be a fabulous category of venues to check out, and prices may be far lower than in peak skiing season!

ing fine dining, indoor pools, spa treatments, and adventures to embark upon in the resort area.

Ski resorts don't always have to be booked in the winter, so let me add the beauty of a ski resort in the off-season, such as in autumn before the snow arrives, with fall foliage all around and no worries about ice or storms as you and your group venture out for winery tours, brewery tastings, shopping, and fall-themed spa treatments for those who wish to have some Me time.

So think about your formality and favorite styles shown here and that you've come up with on your own, and think about how you want your wedding to feel for you and for your guests. And you'll be on your way to the next big choices.

2

Deciding on Your Destination Wedding Date

Choosing the perfect date for your destination wedding is so very important to your wedding vision, as well as your process in planning it. As with most important things, there is not just one factor in this decision. Here, we'll sort through the many facets of wedding date choosing for any type of destination wedding, near or far.

1. *The amount of time you need to plan it.* On average, according to The Wedding Report (a survey site sharing stats about the wedding industry), the average amount of time spent planning a wedding—any type of wedding—is 14 months. While there are lots of votes in that survey for 3–6 months, 6–9 months, and even under 3 months (whew!), the importance here is that you have adequate time that works with your personal schedule to do a ton of researching, hiring, planning, and—this is important—perhaps making the time to pre-visit your chosen venue

to meet with your on-site wedding team in person, tour sites on the property and envision your wedding and wedding weekend . . . and also get a romantic escape with your partner. You have to strike a perfect balance in the time you'll spend planning, or you could suffer stress and wasted money on a "rush job" or—just as dangerous to your sanity and to your budget—have too much time to reconsider your decisions, losing heart for some early decisions, changing them, losing deposits, and overwhelming yourself. So get realistic about the block of time you'll need to pull this off.

2. *When you have the time to go.* You know the busy season at your job, those months when you have to turn down every social invitation because it's your busy time, and you're clocking twelve-hour days. If you're a teacher, you know when you have off of work during the summer months. First, ask yourself how many days you'd like to plan for your destination wedding. Would you be happy with flying in only the day before, sharing a weekend with your guests, and then flying home right after your wedding (opting to take a delayed honeymoon, as is a current trend for all wedding types)? Or would you like to fly in a few days before the wedding, maybe get a full day with your bridal party who also fly in early, spend three days with your guests, then go on your weeklong

Planning Tips

You'd be surprised to know how many couples fight about their vacation days. "Because you had to go to Vegas for Tom's bachelor party, now you don't have enough vacation days for our wedding! We have to wait so long now! I told you not to go!" Yes, that's a stress-induced argument that is particularly fiery because it's a guilt trip as well. So make an agreement not to give each other trouble about past use of vacation days. Reaching into the past for a weapon isn't a good thing for your partnership at any time, let alone while planning your wedding.

honeymoon? Or two-week honeymoon? Now is when you decide on the length of your stay, so that you can match that time-off need with your wishes. You'll have to have the vacation days available. How do your and your partner's vacation day tallies look right now? Do the ones you have for this year expire at the end of the year, or do they roll over for next year? Have you taken a bunch of your vacation days already this year, and find yourself with a shortage for your possible destination wedding at the end of the year? Add 'em up, and see how your available time off stands.

3. *When it's a good time at your destination.* This is where you have to do a lot of research on locations in order to find out about their peak season. Peak season is when the destination is the most crowded, likely due to its ideal weather. Peak season is when all attractions in the area are open and available to you. It's the region's "on" time, when demand is high. Low season is when the destination is less popular, less crowded, less expensive in most cases. It may also be when certain businesses and attractions in the area are closed, so keep in mind that the "ghost town" feel is real, and that some of the things you may want to do during your stay might not be available. "Shoulder season" is right in the middle, usually when everything's open, the weather is still ideal, and perhaps prices are a bit lower because it's not in top demand and not as crowded. These seasons are important to check out because they'll impact every element of your wedding. Ask the event planner at your destination to fill you in on peak, shoulder, and low seasons to help you choose the perfect wedding date for your wishes. And let's not forget hurricane and storm season, which can threaten your big day in every way, from upsetting travel plans, causing you to cancel your wedding, or your group winding up in a crowded storm cellar or shelter while the storm of the century rages outside. For the Caribbean islands, hurricane season runs from June to November, for instance, so you'll find in many locations that late November through May has better odds of storm scarcity.

Planning Tips

Check out the travel and tourism websites for any destination you have in mind. Most will have a section on their peak times as well as information on their low seasons and storm seasons. Don't see that on their site? Call the tourism department to find out, and while you're on the phone with them, mention that you're a wedding group that may be coming to their location. Many tourism departments have "welcome packs" for wedding groups that can include coupons and tickets to area attractions as well as fun little gifts for your stay. Only take the pack, though, if you've decided on that location for sure. And check with your hotel or resort. Some close down completely during storm season, regularly shuttered for the fall months.

Other concerns about the location's season: heat and humidity—which can make for a steamy, uncomfortable wedding—and their bug season, which in some locations means the presence of bugs that are just part of the deal at that time of year. You may find yourselves sleeping beneath mosquito nets or trying to get that prehistoric-looking flying bug out of your room at night.

And then there's the issue of spring break. Those kids have come to the location for a reason: the weather is perfect, hotels are offering deals to attract them, and there's lots to do in the area. Noisy, partying crowds are everywhere, and drunk and disorderly behavior is all around. You likely know this is not your dream situation for your wedding, so re-familiarize yourself with when spring break takes place so that you can plan accordingly. And while winter breaks don't have the same big reputation that spring break does, those, too, are going to bring in big crowds of partiers, as well as lots of families who will be everywhere at your location. Winter break has become a big time for family reunions. Any high demand time can pose some limitations to your day.

Lastly, festivals. Big ones you've heard of and big ones you haven't heard of, all of which bring big crowds, concerts, noise, and often, higher prices. Ask your resort about any festivals planned for the time you're looking at, and also check online event calendars for the destinations you have in mind.

4. *When it's a good time in your group.* If you have a relative undergoing treatment for an illness, it's something to keep in mind. Think about travel issues for those who are pregnant; will they be very pregnant and unable to travel at the time of your wedding, or will they have a newborn at your chosen time? It may be best to choose a wedding date that puts them in the clear, and allows you to have your best friend or sister at your wedding. We'll get more into your guests' needs when we're tackling wedding locations, but think about your loved ones' life situations now to help you determine your ideal destination wedding date.

5. *And of course, availability at your wedding location.* They'll need to have your wedding date open, and enough availability for your guests to book rooms. Here's an important question to ask: Is your reservation guaranteed when you book it? I'm hearing about some shady stuff out there, in which a hotel books a wedding, then calls back a few months later to say your reservation has been canceled because a corporation or large wedding has booked out the entire place. Can you imagine?

That's something to guard yourself against, and while mishaps may never be able to be fully avoided, at least you'll have it on record in an e-mail that you asked about the hotel's policy in this matter. Sorry to scare you, but this is something that does happen, so best to protect yourself as best you can.

There's also another issue you might find yourself facing. A friend or relative might have a wedding booked for a weekend near your hoped-for wedding date. It would be a challenge for your shared guests to fly across the planet to that wedding, then fly across the planet the other way to get to your wedding. So collect up all of those Save the Dates you've received for friends' and loved ones' weddings and big events, and steer clear as much as possible. This is why it's advised to send out your Save the Dates far in advance, at least sixteen weeks or more, to get on everyone's calendars and block off that time for your big event.

Keep in mind that your destination wedding planner will likely know your chosen location well and can advise about potential wedding dates. He or she might know that a certain month is more temperate for a wedding, sharing a tale about guests getting sunburned just ten minutes into a destination wedding ceremony, heat stroke taking guests down, and guests burning their fingers on the utensils set at the guest tables. These are things wedding planners know, and their input is so valuable. You don't want to be the wedding where someone's kid got a third-degree burn from a metal chair and will be scarred for life. So tap into the experience of a pro, and that pro may be able to work some magic to get you booked at a venue that's tough to book during peak season.

Wedding Etiquette Tips

For a destination wedding, six months is more like it for your Save-the-Date sends.

The Day of the Week

An important issue when it comes to setting the foundation for your destination wedding. Imagine hearing, "All of our weekend dates are booked at our hotel this year, but we have a Wednesday open!" from your resort's wedding planner. What do you do? The alternative is waiting another year for your wedding and grabbing a Saturday then. And a Wednesday wedding costs half the price of a weekend wedding. That's attractive.

But what about your wedding guests who have to take time off of work to travel and be present for your wedding? A Wednesday is a challenge for them, and perhaps for you. But that half-price cost! What will you do? More couples are grabbing the Wednesday date these days, since a half-price wedding is so enticing. Guests may be resentful, and some guests may not be able to come. That's your burden here when you pick a weekday. So give it some thought, because those weekdays may be more available and more budget-friendly.

If you do choose a weekend, decide between Friday, Saturday, and Sunday, of course. Some guests will fly in Friday night after work and leave Sunday. Some will daringly fly in on Saturday to attend your wedding and leave the next day.

I spoke with wedding planners at several resorts who told me that some of their weekday weddings are attended by the wedding couple, their immediate families, and a few friends. The couple wanted it that way, they say. They didn't want to obligate all of their friends and family, and they didn't want to pay for a one-hundred-person guest list. Twelve suited them just fine. So there's an option for those of you who don't face the "what will guests want?" issue. You may want it to be just your core circle at your destination wedding, and plan a "reception" back home later. Which is a viable option, now that more resorts are offering special packages for what they call mini weddings. That package may include three hotel rooms in the wedding package, so none of your core circle guests have to pay for their rooms. Or perhaps you get the free room and they get a discount. Check into those small wedding packages, since they can be budget-saving gold and headache-saving gold as well.

The Time of Your Wedding

It's all about the light. There are couples who want a ceremony perfectly timed to the sunset over the ocean, some who love the twilight glow in that Italian countryside town, some who want their wedding to be lit up magically in the dark of night, and some who find sunrise to be symbolic perfection for their new life. So let's look into time of day for your destination wedding a little bit more, since there are some extra issues you might not have considered.

* *Morning Weddings:* They might actually be at sunrise, with quiet all around and a smart way to dodge the issue of a resort full of vacationers. That means fewer people gawking, photo-bombing, sneaking a bite from the buffet, and—less cynically—wishing you well from a respectful distance. Morning weddings invite lavish brunch buffets and attendant-manned food stations, dessert spreads that surprise and delight, champagne and mimosas or tropical drinks that are completely OK to enjoy since you're on vacation! The day will begin extra-early for you, perhaps way before the sun rises for your getting ready time, but you get the whole of the day to enjoy celebrating your early morning vows. The sun isn't strong, morning breezes flutter by, and the colors of the early morning sky have their own majesty (while sunsets often get all the praise!). Your ceremony commences, your reception stretches to afternoon, and the beautiful hours of evening and night stretch out before you for relaxed together time with your loved ones. A perfect opportunity for an evening sail or an after-party informally at the resort's lounge.
* *Afternoon Weddings:* The sun's been up for a while and temperatures are increasing. Depending on where you've gone for your destination wedding—tropical island, city, ski resort, and more—an afternoon wedding might be traditional lunchtime of noon, or it may start at 3:00 p.m. or so. A cocktail party suits this time of wedding, with light bites and hot hors d'oeuvres circulating among your cocktail-sipping crowd, a buffet, or a

Think About Your Guests

What's the best time of day for your guests? If you know that your parents and grandparents turn in early, will it be ideal for you to go out into town without them? Or do you want your early-to-bed crowd to be able to join in comfortably with the entirety of your celebration, which they could do with a morning or afternoon wedding? Think about the heat of the day, or cold of the day as your destination may present. What's the most comfortable temperature for your wedding? Talk to your planner: locations nearer to the equator can present higher-than-expected sunburn risk, which guests might not be familiar with. Sunblock is necessary at any time of day, but at peak sun, risk is greater.

sit-down luncheon with a customized menu of delectable dishes. Sunset illuminates the close of your wedding, ideal for photos, and there's plenty of nighttime left for an after-party.

• *Evening Weddings:* Starting at 5:00 p.m.–8:00 p.m., evening weddings bring in lighting effects to illuminate your ceremony and/or reception, and an open-air sky lets guests see that magnificent sky full of stars above you. A tent may welcome outdoor entertainment and dining, or you might choose a ballroom or restaurant indoor setting, with invitation for guests to wander outside to seating areas with their drinks. In some regions, nighttime nature sounds add to the ambience of the wedding. Reaching to the resort's curfew—which may be 10:00 p.m., so be sure to ask!—your group can continue on to an after-party, to the resort's bar, or into town for late-night partying.

3

Deciding on Your Destination Wedding Budget

LET'S CLEAR UP one misconception in the wedding realm right off the bat: having a small wedding does not always mean your budget will be smaller. So you can forget about all of that advice you see on wedding budget blog posts about how cutting your guest list is a way to ensure a lower budget. Not true at all. Depending upon your chosen location and your decisions about catering, drinks, décor, entertainment, photography and videography, and so many other wedding elements, you could have a $100,000 wedding with a guest list of just ten people. Sure, your per-person expenses for catering could be ten times the cost, but that doesn't mean you couldn't go big with all of the other details and rocket up your expenses.

If you haven't looked into vendor prices yet, brace yourself for numbers that can be jaw-dropping to you. But then think about how important their services are for this once-in-a-lifetime event, how their work helps to create your dream day in the highest quality possible, and—this may be the most important factor—how their experience and knowledge of the million moving parts in this big undertaking can save you from stress headaches and budget waste. You can't put a price tag on that.

Now, that said, let's get working on your destination wedding budget.

Where Is Your Wedding Money Coming From?

Before you start breathing into a paper bag to calm yourself as you face the money aspect of planning your dream destination wedding, let's figure out how much you'll realistically be able to spend. Are you among the many couples who start saving for their wedding for a year or two in advance? I'm seeing couples setting wedding dates several years in the future so that they can afford more of the weddings they want. If you haven't started saving, there's no time like the present. Set up an interest-bearing savings account and shovel monthly deposits into it.

Do you get tax refunds? If so, consider putting all, most, or some of your tax refund money into your wedding savings account. Some couples find themselves facing down a change to what they normally do with their tax refunds. If you're among those who opt to pay down their credit cards with this windfall, you can create your own split with your refund. Use some to pay down a card or two, then put the rest in your wedding savings. Smart decisions both ways. If you usually go wild with your tax refund, spending it on a shopping spree or taking a vacation, this year, you might want to skip those treats and funnel your refund into your wedding savings instead. There will be plenty of years to buy shoes and to go on vacations in the future, as a married couple who had a great wedding.

Is there any way to make more money at your job? I know, this one sounds a bit unrealistic, when you're already working so hard and finding it tough to get time for yourself. But there may be some opportunities for overtime, time and a half for working a holiday, and bonuses from your extra effort on the job. Depending upon your career, some of these bonuses and extra pay projects can deliver mightily, and perhaps make you look amazing to the bosses. Promotion, anyone?

Budget Tip

I love this tip, which was inspired by a *Sports Illustrated Swimsuit Edition* supermodel. (I know, but just stick with me here!) The supermodel had to pose in a swimsuit on a frozen tundra in below-zero temperature, while a helicopter flew up and around her to get that perfect shot for the magazine. The cold and wind were intense. When asked how she could bear that freezing wind, she said she just imagined how much money she was making by the minute and that made it worth it. Now here's how that supermodel's advice helps your budget, should you decide to work some extra hours or take on a big project for bonus pay: look at each minute's or hour's earnings as working toward some part of your wedding. After a tiring few hours of overtime, you can warm up your mood by knowing you just paid for your wedding programs, your favors, a gift for one of your bridesmaids, or one of the bouquets. Look at the budget chart at the back of this book and pick out all of the small-money items you'll need for your wedding day. Or the individual items in a larger category (like bouquets in general). Make a list of those items and their costs, and carry that list with you. When you're working to make extra money for your wedding, you can look at that list and say, "Just paid for our wedding license!" or "Just paid for one tier of our wedding cake!" It'll put a smile on your face and return you to feeling confident about managing your budget one day—or one workday—at a time.

Now let's talk about the advice you've heard about not running up your credit cards to pay for your wedding. That's good advice, since it's never a good idea to dig yourself into a hole of debt for your wedding, which would lead you to spending years paying so much more than you spent to get your cards back in good shape and your credit score nice and high. And you definitely don't want to jam up your credit cards without your partner knowing about it. Financial infidelity is a big Don't in wedding planning and in marriage as well.

But if you manage your cards well, paying off handsome amounts as you go, you could earn airline miles, gift cards, and other perks from your purchases. And these things can go toward your wedding expenses. So when you're in the supermarket at 7:00 a.m. in your yoga outfit and a ponytail, buying yogurt, you're just like that supermodel "earning" rewards by the minute for your wedding. With the right credit card rewards plan, and of course your smarts in paying your card down as you go, some of your wedding elements and possibly your travel could be free.

Will your parents pay for any portion of your wedding? This is a big one, since parents may expect that if they're paying for wedding plans, they get to chime in on them, too. So before you broach the subject with any of your parents, have a conversation about how you'll handle the plan. You know your parents best, and while you might not have ever been in a situation where money was involved (all the more powerful because so much emotion is involved), you know their style when it comes to sharing plans. The "tryout" may have been co-planning a holiday

Budget Tip

Just be sure you're keeping track of when your credit card rewards can be used, and how, and when they expire. Choose your cards wisely as well, and understand the terms. It's extra research, but important organization steps to take.

dinner, or your engagement party. If they got power-hungry then, you know you'll likely face the same control issues. So proceed wisely.

Figure out the best wording for how you'll ask parents about their financial participation in the wedding plans. You're hitting Start on an important dynamic for your wedding when you do, so consider, "We're starting to think about our wedding plans, and we wanted to ask if and how you'd like to participate." Short, sweet, and to the point. Your parents have likely discussed what they'd like to do for your wedding, and they may have a plan. They've just been waiting for you to open the door. You may hear, "We were thinking of giving you a check for X dollars to use however you'd like." You may hear, "We'd like to pay for the bar tab and the cake, if that's all right with you." When you do hear an offer about particular wedding details they'd like to pay for, don't miss the opportunity to set the parameters now, such as with, "Thank you! That would be terrific, and it'll be such fun going to the cake tasting with you!" Parents then know what to expect, without having to ask.

It's all about setting realistic expectations for parents and for anyone else, like grandparents, who may wish to chip in for the wedding plans.

Now let's say that your parents respond with, "Yes, we'll be happy to help out," and they say nothing else. That probably means they don't know how much they can give just yet, so a response of "OK, whenever you're ready, we can talk about what you'd like to do." It's always best to have the conversation when everyone is ready for it. Be patient, even if you really want to start booking everything now. If you push, warning parents that the best venues book up quickly, that can create an anxiety or resentment in your parents. Remember, a great wedding is all about how everyone feels, and the same is true for your parents' involvement in the planning process. Your feelings count as well. So don't rush the conversation, don't rush the plans. Give parents the freedom to check out their money situation and get back to you.

Another smart source is your wedding gift registry. While debates rage on about whether or not you can put a note on your personal wedding website, asking for cash to pay off your student loans, buy a house, or pay for your honeymoon—

and these debates get heated between old-school etiquette folks and new-era thinkers who just see a way to get it done—it's still dicey to ask for cash. But here's where we're at: guests are happy to give you a gift you would really like and need, and they're finding that a gift card is the perfect solution. A gift card may help you get décor for your weddings, perhaps even your dress, and gift card fusions like HoneyFund.com can help you with travel arrangement costs *and* shopping, since your gift card gives you lots of choices in how the funds may be used.

The last budget foundational tip is listing up what you can get for free. That means any freebies included in the wedding package you select, any wedding items you can borrow from a friend (like a sign or other décor item), and anything that comes free from your rewards points. There's a psychological perk to mastering your budget when you know you're able to acquire some details without using it.

Throughout this book, you'll find boxed tips on budget-saving ideas, so flag or tag those to help you make smart decisions that make the most of your budget as a whole without sacrificing quality or causing regrets (or disasters!).

4

Deciding on Your
Destination Wedding Guest List

You've already started thinking about the size of wedding you'd like, and while your budget may be a big factor, it's also important to think about the experience you'd like to have at your wedding. A small wedding with a few guests gives you more time to spend with each of them, and may also allow you to have your wedding at certain venues with smaller capacities, such as a tiny stone chapel in an Italian village, or on a private yacht in the Mediterranean that accommodates twenty guests on board. A larger wedding with one hundred plus people may mean that in the fast-paced itinerary of your big day, you only get a few minutes of quality time with each. And that lovely stone chapel is off your possibilities list. Multiple factors work together here.

So let's start building your destination wedding guest list, using the pages at the back of this book to help you with your all-important organization. Begin by thinking about tiers of guests. Like a five-tiered wedding cake, only it's people you're counting, not layers of cake. I'm providing a sample Tiers List here so that you can see how it works, but please do feel free to switch some tiers around. Your friends may be more important for you to have there than your aunts and uncles (although you'd never say that to them!).

- *Tier 1:* the two of you, your parents and stepparents, grandparents, siblings, and their partners and kids, your bridal party and their guests
- *Tier 2:* aunts and uncles, cousins and their partners/guests/kids
- *Tier 3:* closest friends and their partners/kids
- *Tier 4:* extended family, such as second cousins and their guests
- *Tier 5:* bosses, work friends, and their guests
- *Tier 6:* more distant friends with whom you'd like to reconnect

And other tiers as you see fit.

This isn't your final guest list. You're just brainstorming here, and there are other possible lists to keep in mind, such as your parents' guest lists. Parents today, regardless of whether or not they're paying for the wedding, will often seek to invite their closest friends—especially if their closest friends invited them to their own kids' weddings—relatives and business associates. So you'll have to pre-plan how you'll handle this issue with them. It's best to inform them right at the start about your wishes for guest list size, given the experience you'd like to have with a smaller or larger guest list. When you approach them with, "We strongly feel that a smaller guest list of under thirty people will give us all the best wedding experience and more quality time with our guests, as well as opening up some terrific, smaller venues," they get your parameters up front.

Now, if you do plan to allow your parents a number of personal invites, decide on that number. Will it be two? three? five? Make it the same rule for both sides, since nothing creates a firestorm and long-lasting power struggles in your happily-ever-after like favoritism of one side. If you have one set of parents able to help pay for the wedding, and the other set unable to pay, that opens up a squeaky door of trouble. Again, keeping guest list allowances even can ward off potentially catastrophic troubles down the line. So call it a "space thing" for your venue interest to help both sides understand.

Can We Bring Our Kids?

The next issue to tackle for your guest list is whether or not to include kids. Talk about another squeaky door of trouble! Many guests don't travel without their kids. Many guests won't wish to or be able to have someone watch their kids for three or four days. Many guests see weddings as a rare chance for the extended family to meet their kids for the first time. If Great-Aunt Harriet will be there, cousin Maria may want her to meet her four kids. And the good news is that guests can bring their kids to your destination to meet Aunt Harriet. But they'll be at the

Planning Tip

Remember that parents are valuable sources of family diplomacy information. They may suggest guests you completely forgot about, saving you from etiquette disasters.

kids' camp at the resort during the wedding, if you've decided on an adults-only wedding experience. If your jaw just dropped because you would never expect kids to stay elsewhere while everyone else parties at your reception, then you know where you stand on the issue. (See what I did there?)

You are in a winning spot because you do have an answer for the guests who request to bring their kids along: there are activities at the resort for all of the kids, and guests are welcome to bring their own sitters along. Many families bring their au pairs and nannies along on trips like this, for their kids to have a familiar, responsible person taking care of them. The kids can attend pre-wedding events while the au pair gets some time by the pool, if he or she prefers. Older cousins who want to make some good money might volunteer to watch the kids during the wedding, rather than attend. And many families will bring along the kids' grandparents to take on the child-care duties while guests enjoy the celebration. Lots of options, ones you can outline on your personal wedding website to head off all of those calls you would otherwise get.

Destination Wedding Etiquette Tip

Keep in mind that you don't have to abide by outdated etiquette rules that say you have to make a blanket rule of all kids versus *no* kids invited. Guests today get it that you're going to have your siblings' kids, or your own kids, in attendance, so they don't have a leg to stand on for any argument based on all or none. Just beware of tricky situations in which you let some guests who beg for their kids to be invited to do so, while others drive their kids to a relative's house prior to the wedding. You don't want simmering resentment and again any whiff of favoritism to sour your wedding. When pushy guests push, stick to your guns with a genuine, "I'm sorry to have to say no. We completely understand, but we've had to make this difficult decision after a lot of thought, and we've already told some guests no, so we can't make any exceptions. But we have some ways to help on our personal wedding website. I can send you the link, if you'd like." Some guests might get indignant; some might not come (using this as their excuse, perhaps). But you need to draw the line where it works best for you.

Can I Bring a Date?

Ah, the dreaded +1. I wish I could say that those wedding blogs purporting that wedding guests are happier now to attend without dates (since weddings are great places to meet other singles!) are on the mark, but that's not always the case. Like most wedding couples before you, you may face the difficult task of trying to decide who gets a +1 and who doesn't. If you attempt to make a rule that only guests in long-standing relationships get a +1, how do you decide what exactly is a long-standing relationship? Five years? A year? Engaged couples only? What about your cousin who has been with her partner for twenty years and hasn't gotten engaged versus your cousin who got engaged to some guy she met on the Internet six months ago? It's dicey stuff here.

But the bottom line is that you get to decide. I like to tell couples in this situation that they can create a new rule of their own: "We're only giving 'plus ones' to couples with whom we have socialized." So that lets you off the hook with the friend whose relatively new boyfriend you really like, and consider a friend, because he has made time for you in his life. You know the guy, and you like him. Compare that to the friend who has a relatively new boyfriend you've never met, and you haven't seen that friend very often, either. They haven't made time for you, and you have no personal connection to that boyfriend. Again, that guest might get offended and might not come to your wedding, but you've drawn a line to make sure your wedding weekend is filled only with people who are special to you.

Now let's talk about B-list guests. They're the people who will get invitations after the first Regrets have come in from your upper tier guests.

It's possible to grant B-list spots to +1s for guests who graciously said they will attend without giving you any hassles about their relatively new boyfriends being invited. Good behavior gets rewarded. Should you B-list anyone? Again, that's up to you, and may be a good idea if you have a guaranteed minimum guest list you're paying for and seeing your response cards coming in with a lot of Regrets. What's a guaranteed minimum guest list? It's the number of guests your venue states as the minimum they will plan for, and that *you'll* pay for. So if your guaranteed minimum guest list is fifty, and you only have forty-four Yes RSVPs, it can be smarter to hand out +1s to fill the void, and avoid diplomacy issues with closer friends and family. Does that mean that other singles who don't get a +1 won't be angry? No, they'll figure out that someone else got something that they didn't, and they may still be resentful. You can't make everyone happy, but you can do your best.

Elderly, Pregnant, and Health-Challenged Guests

You'll just have to make sure your venues are accessible to them, and that your guests know everything they need to know about reaching your venue, as well as medical facilities nearby. That latter one is important. Help any challenged guests to find out all they need to know about attending safely; don't just leave it to them to search.

The Issue with Work Friend Invitations

Be careful about over-inviting "have to" guests, such as in the event of wanting to invite a few of your close work friends but feeling like you then have to invite all of your colleagues, your bosses, and all of their guests. These obligation invites may turn into a disappointment for your wedding experience when fewer of your family and close friends can attend your destination wedding . . . but all of those colleagues you rarely talk to can make it, looking forward to a vacation with all of their food, drink, and activities paid for by you. Your wedding can then feel like a work retreat. And when you also invite other obligation friends you barely have a connection to—perhaps because you were invited to their weddings a long time ago, but haven't talked to since—you could wind up at your wedding surrounded by people you barely know and all of their dates. It doesn't make for a warm, intimate wedding experience when you have no idea who half of your guests are.

How to Be OK with Regrets

Just thought you'd like a little boost with regard to any response cards you receive with the disappointing news that some guests will not be able to attend your wedding. Please don't take it personally. Some people are so jammed with their work and family schedules that they couldn't attend a wedding a block away from their house, let alone fly across the planet for your big day. Some people can't step away from their own overwhelming responsibilities, like caring for a sick parent or child, or keeping up at their job in order to keep their job. So don't do yourself the disservice of making assumptions, seeing Regrets as signs that you are not loved, or that your wedding isn't important to people. And please don't measure love by reciprocals, thinking that if you took the time to travel to someone else's wedding, they should take the time to travel to yours.

People have limitations they'd rather not have. For the vast majority of your loved ones, it was simply a matter of not being able to attend. Now, let me help you avoid even more unnecessary disappointment. Let's say you see on social media that the people who said they couldn't go to your wedding because they were busy with work were . . . at a weekend getaway, or at a neighbor's party. I've heard from wedding couples who branded those now ex-friends liars and terrible people. But it may have just been that those "terrible people" really needed to take a few hours away from caring for a parent or child, or from their crushing work responsibilities. Or maybe the work project deadline got pushed back the day before, so they grabbed the chance to escape life stress to recharge for a little while. The danger of social media is that it can lead to assumptions and hurt feelings. So if you see one of those "oh really!?" posts, give them and yourself a break. They missed your amazing wedding, and you're not going to spend your first newlywed days stressing about a perceived betrayal.

You never know what's going on behind the scenes in someone's life. Maybe your friend just found out she's pregnant, and her doctor told her not to travel. In a few months, she'll share her big news with the world. Maybe your cousins are having a big struggle with finances. They're not going to share that secret with you. It could be anything, but whatever it is keeping them from being with you, send them good wishes and positive vibes to overcome whatever might be challenging them. That includes last-minute cancellations as well. Be a bigger thinker than one who takes it personally. Keep your experience positive. Time will tell if that person isn't worth keeping in your close satellite. Raging about it now only makes you the thief of your own joy.

So take responses with a grain of salt, and focus instead on those who will be joining you.

5

Deciding on Your Destination Wedding Location

DECIDING WHERE TO go for your destination is an exciting step in this process, and in addition to looking at dreamy photos of a tropical island or snowy mountainous region, you're also looking at a number of other things. For instance, if your choice of wedding location is Hawaii, you're making a decision that you and all of your guests will need to travel to Hawaii. If you want a snowy, mountainous wedding, you could go any number of places, from the Alps to the Catskill Mountains in New York. If you dream of a fall wedding with all of its leafy colors, you will likely have a large range of locations to choose from, such as New England to a resort an hour from your home (an hour's drive counts as a destination wedding, after all!).

So understanding that the image you seek could be found in any number of locations near or far, let's start breaking down the process of choosing your destination wedding location.

- *Decide if it's a scene you want, or a particular place.* Knowing you want a beach wedding is not the same as knowing you want a beach wedding at the beach where you've always vacationed, or where you got engaged. There are beaches everywhere in the world, but one beach may be special to you. Does a particular location mean a lot to you? That will point you in its direction. Is it just the beach scenery you're interested in? You could look at many different beach locations, again, overseas or domestic.

- *Decide how far you want to travel.* And how far your guests will have to travel. Some couples don't give this a second thought. It's the Seychelles or nothing. Some couples do consider distance, but to them, a flight to Europe is not the same as flying halfway around the world. Europe is no big deal. It's one flight. Not four. With sleeping pods on some airlines now, such a long flight can be quite comfortable. And then there are couples who don't want their destination wedding to be too far away. They want it to be affordable and more easily do-able for them and for their guests. They don't want anyone losing a day to travel on either side of their wedding. And they want to be able to take at least one scouting trip to their location before the big day. A closer location would make that more feasible for them. Some couples opt to avoid the passport issue by planning a destination wedding within the United States.

- *Decide how much you want to spend.* A farther-away destination can mean higher travel costs, higher phone bills, higher shipping costs. For your wedding budget, this can be crushing. So, too, can it be crushing for your wedding guests, who may find it a strain on their own budgets just to get to your location . . . and then they feel money stress while they're there, not being able financially to enjoy as many dining, play, and spa opportunities as they would like while they're in such a great location. Even at an all-inclusive resort, where everything is covered, they may wish they could go out on the town with other guests without worrying about their credit card limits. (Now keep in mind that a nearby resort can cost three times what a faraway resort costs, so it's going to take some research time for this one.)

- *Decide on how easy you want your marriage application process to be.* In the Legalities chapter, you'll soon find out that it can be very challenging to arrange for a valid marriage license in some locations. Each country, island, city, and town has its own rules regarding paperwork, timing, fees, blood tests, and other *musts* before they'll issue a marriage license in order for your marriage to be legal. When you start looking into these requirements, your choice of location might be swayed by avoiding places where there are a ton of rules (or impossibilities). One of the biggest rules is a residency requirement that could require you to stay in your location for a week or several months before your wedding.
- *Decide on the season or weather you'd like.* Some locations are in full floral bloom during certain months, sunny but less humid in other months, scorching hot in other months, or rainy and monsoon-ish in other seasons. For instance, Hawaii has its rainy season between November and March, which might make your big day a washout. While you can never predict the weather, you may want to steer clear of some locations during hurricane season.
- *Decide on peak season vs. off-season.* Choosing your location can come down to choosing for its busyness, seasonal pricing, and weather. If you have the perfect window of time for your destination wedding getaway, you might choose your location by this factor. Off-season could make things quieter and less crowded, but some sites might not be open and the weather might not be optimal. Peak season could offer all you want, including ideal weather as the norm, never mind the higher prices and bigger crowds. Consider your location choices' off- and peak-seasons to help you decide, based on what you want your experience to be like. Some couples don't want any part of having spring breakers at their resort, for instance, not to mention increased traffic or the restaurants and shops in the area being shuttered for the off-season.
- *Decide on the energy level you'd like.* Some locations, like Las Vegas or New York City, are high-energy and active all the time. And some locations are very still and quiet. Some couples need their privacy, and want a resort

all to themselves. Some are fine with being one of several weddings taking place at a resort at the same time. Choosing your location can come down to how you'd like the place to feel, and how you feel being there. If you're always unnerved by crowds, lights, and noise, you'll be more comfortable at a quieter location.

* *Decide if you want an all-inclusive resort.* We'll get into picking resorts specifically soon, but I wanted to be sure you knew about this category, since not all locations have all-inclusive resorts that are of the highest quality possible. You might find that the location you have in mind, such as an island, doesn't have any all-inclusives at all. Which means you'll face a different set of tasks and costs if you do choose a location without one. If you know you want an all-inclusive resort or hotel, that will narrow down your location search results.

How Do You Find These Things Out?

Personal experience is always best. You might decide that a resort you stayed at while you were dating, perhaps where you got engaged, is definitely The One for your destination wedding location. You love the setting, the service, the spa, the sea activities, and the cuisine and drinks. You may have been there half a dozen

Thinking About Your Guests

If you know the place, you know what your guests will enjoy. If you know the morning champagne breakfast sail is amazing, plan an outing for your group. If you know a great restaurant near your big city hotel, that's where your rehearsal dinner can be. Don't worry about outdoing those friends or relatives whose weddings took place there. No one compares as much as you might think.

times, loving it more and more each time, and you can't think of another place that would be more perfect. You want to share it with your friends and family.

When you know the place, you know more of what you can expect. You might have stayed at a resort for a friend's or relative's destination wedding, and it's not in any way a Don't to choose the same location. Your friend or cousin who married there will be flattered that you love their wedding spot, and they'll relish the chance to go back again.

Asking friends who married away—but you either weren't invited or couldn't attend—is also a great idea, since they now know how the location performs for weddings. They may be able to clue you in to some things you have to plan or have to steer clear of, helping you to perhaps the perfect choice.

Friends and family who have vacationed at a fab-looking place recently can also be great sources of information. They may have attended a destination wedding there, or were just there on vacation, but they can be priceless sources of intel on the spot and on surrounding areas to check out.

Look online. Not just at wedding website articles that may have been written by staffers or bloggers who were invited on press visits, treated to the good life, and given preferential treatment (by resort employees who knew how important their reviews would be!). This is not to say that staffers and bloggers' insights aren't important. Most have a lot of journalistic integrity. But their experience might have been a bit different from what you can expect. Look as well at magazines' Best Of and Top 10 lists of resorts and locations. *Travel and Leisure* is just one magazine with impressive best of and awards lists for a large number of locations and categories.

Can you trust online reviews? That's always been a big question for wedding couples. I'd say to look through them for specific details, but keep in mind that some people who experience less than they want are often quick to post harsh reviews. Some may be vague. And some may give you excellent details to consider. They're worth reading through, just for added input.

Tourist board websites will give you the details on what you'll need for a marriage license, as well as listings of various hotels, restaurants, and attractions. But

Planning Tip

Be sure to check out the hashtag #Engage17, #Engage18, and so on, with the last two numbers corresponding to the year. This is the hashtag for a stellar wedding planner event/conference that is held at amazing resorts several times a year. When you look at these Instagram posts and other social media tags, you'll get to see lots of details from the event, including mentions of the resort where these in-the-know wedding planners are learning, dining, and partying.

keep in mind that some places appear on the tourism board website because they paid to be featured there. While it seems like a tourist board would want to show only the cream of the crop in their region's offerings, it may be likely that advertising is a factor.

Wedding planners know the best locations. They may have planned events there before, or they know other planners who have. And planners are chatty with each other. They'll rave about a fabulous location, and they'll gripe about a crummy one with no holds barred. A wedding planner's inside information from colleagues—including others like photographers—is priceless information, and can further connect you to the best vendors in the area as well. Your planner can also dig up information on locations he or she hasn't heard of before, nor has anyone in their circle. Planners belong to professional associations, linking them to thousands upon thousands of accredited professionals all over the world. They can easily find out reputable opinions from their colleagues, which may save the day in directing you to a great location, or save the day by steering you away from a notoriously negative one.

Again, we'll get more into assessing individual properties in a later chapter. We're just setting your focus on the general location of your wedding right now.

6

The Resort's Wedding Planner vs. Your Own Wedding Planner

YOUR WEDDING PLANNER is going to be so important to the success of your destination wedding, as well as to your own wellness level while planning it. A great wedding coordinator brings so many skills to the table, from negotiating, to assessing vendors and packages, to understanding all of the super-fine print in contracts, keeping you and your budget on track, and rescuing your wedding when a last-minute fix has to be found. Destination weddings present special challenges, since you're not a short drive away from your venue and vendors, and some chosen locations introduce language and cultural hurdles to handle. So if you wish to use the Fairy Godmother (or Fairy Godfather) analogy for your wedding planner's seemingly magical effects and work, it certainly fits!

I've mentioned often in this book so far, and will do so again, that a wedding planner is an essential. While you may think you have the time and ability to plan your own wedding from afar, it's a big fact that wedding planners know the inner workings of each of the industries in the

Planning Tip

Check the list of tasks provided by your site's wedding planner. Not what's included in the package, such as the meal, cake, and photographer, but what the planner will actually work on. Some resorts' wedding planners are actually their catering managers who are referred to as wedding planners. Sure, they plan the reception, and connect you to officiants and other experts known to the resort, but there are a ton of other tasks to be done. The resort's wedding planner might not count it among her responsibilities to plan your group outings, since they have nothing to do with catering. She may not help with your invitations and budget. If a list of planner tasks is not on the resort's website, ask for a list. Never assume that "wedding planner" means all that you think it does. It would be terrible to find out that so many planning tasks are not covered, dumped in your lap, and hard to handle from afar.

wedding field, from floral design to catering to fireworks. And they know the nuances that make a celebration better for all. They're experienced, and not as emotionally invested as you are (although they are emotionally invested in making you happy and your wedding spectacular). So that makes them crucial to handling the thousand moving parts of a destination wedding plan.

All it takes is one wrong move or one detail forgotten by a self-planning couple, and the wedding can take a big hit, perhaps tumbling around them. Some self-planning couples come home from their destination weddings not actually married. And some come home without having the wedding they planned and paid for. Disasters all around.

So let's look deeper into the topic of working with a professional wedding planner, because what you might not know (yet) is that many different types of destination wedding planners exist out there, and some might not be able to do as much as you wish.

On-Site Wedding Planner

The on-site wedding planner at a hotel, resort, or cruise ship is an employee of the hotel, resort, or cruise ship and is very familiar with the site's locations and favorite vendors. They may or may not be accredited wedding planners who received extensive training from a wedding planning association. They may be supremely talented, and their inside knowledge of everything weddings at that location can be a very big benefit to you. Again, you have to make sure that you know what their list of responsibilities is, so that you have no misunderstanding. Some on-site wedding planners may be front desk staffers who love planning weddings and "move over" to become the resort's resident wedding planner. You never know, so you have to check and interview that wedding planner in as much detail as you would interview any wedding planner or vendor.

Check also on the on-site wedding planner's timing for your wedding details. Since he or she may be the sole wedding planner at a large resort, for the sake of that person's efficiency and sanity, you may find that this planner has a rule about dealing with wedding planning just the month before the wedding. Some will help you plan all the way through, and some will not. So be sure you're clear on what to expect.

On-site wedding planners know the work of vendors who have done events at the resort in the past, so those may be the ones recommended to you. You might find that this planner will not participate in finding other outside vendors, and you might also find that outside vendors are not allowed. Each site makes their own rules, so rather than try to fight them, it's best to make sure you understand them.

I'm not trying to turn you away from on-site wedding planners. They have invaluable information and are invested in making sure your wedding comes off without a hitch. Your online reviews of the planner's work reflect on the venue, so they may be held to very high standards by their employer. A guide on the inside can suggest some excellent event ideas, and bring in the perfect musicians or other experts known in that region's wedding community.

On-site planner assistance may be "free," in the sense of being included in your wedding package. Or your site might charge a fee for this expert's work.

Professional Wedding Coordinator in Your Wedding's Location

This expert is a professional wedding planner who is located near your wedding venue, and ideally has planned weddings at your sites in the past. They might be on the resort's list of preferred vendors. You'll always want to work with a professional, accredited wedding or event professional who has received training and perhaps master planner designation from a reputable event planning association, and has many years of experience in your style of wedding.

Take a look at this planner's packages so that you can choose between full wedding planning from start-to-finish, month-of and day-of wedding planning assistance, to pick the package that best meets your needs. For a destination wedding, start-to-finish is the package that will best help you find and hire the best wedding vendors that have to be booked far in advance.

No matter how far away you are, how big your wedding is, or what your budget is, this wedding planner is likely to have a handle on every detail you need. Some planners will even address your invitations for you and help you design your wedding logo. These planners will do it all, including special requests, and I love them for helping you plan surprises for one another. The planner, even from far

Planning Tip

Use Skype and Google Docs to share images and your planning details with far-away wedding planners. Pinterest boards may also be sent, to show the designs you like and your other wedding inspirations. Free online technology can remove the miles between you, allowing you to collaborate efficiently. Some destination wedding couples and their planners set up weekly Skype sessions to keep on top of their tasks, and when multiple people need to connect, Google Hangouts and group Skypes may be terrific options for group chatting.

away, forms a relationship with you and can help with the more personal aspects of your wedding getaway.

This wedding planner is likely to plan all of your outings, and can handle anything that comes up along the way. You will likely have access to this planner's assistants as well, adding even more creative and efficient minds to your team. And again, by virtue of being local to your site, they know all the best vendors for suggestion to you and can steer you away from any unpalatable or unreliable vendors. You may also get personal recommendations of nearby restaurants for your rehearsal dinner and other events from this near-site professional.

A Wedding Planner Near You

It can be a great help to work with a qualified, accredited, professional wedding planner located near you, so that you can meet in person, look at photos together, go to lunch, and form a fabulous working and personal relationship. This local planner can work in tandem with the on-site wedding planner to create a team for your benefit, giving you the best of both worlds. And your local wedding planner can also do a lot of the legwork in finding your perfect on-site vendors and additional event venues. He or she will be your Hometown Hero for your wedding, letting you plan in-person all the way through.

You might prefer this in-person dynamic far more than planning via Skype and sending images back and forth. Your in-person, local planner can present to you live, actual floral arrangement samples and bouquets, hand you linens to feel, and provide lots of sensory experience on your wedding details. This may be more of what you want for your wedding experience.

When your wedding rolls around, you don't leave your local planner behind. It can be very important to fly them in to your wedding location and put them up, so that they may continue their good work on your behalf.

Your planner's work will go beyond connecting with on-site professionals and guests. They can be your liaison with the venue staff, assist with attire, menu, stationery, décor, accommodations and all the other necessary selections/decision making process," says Orsini.

When last-minute snafus arise, and they will, your wedding planner steps in to save the day. Don't forget that a quality wedding professional has a trained eye for potential problems. So if she sees that a beach party setup doesn't have a directional sign to help guests find a nearby bathroom, she'll get one or make one. If she doesn't see the velvet rope you ordered to keep your welcome party private from other hotel guests, she's going to make sure the staff sets it up. If she finds the location to be a hotbed of mosquitoes, she's going to the gift shop to buy out their stock of mosquito repellant for guests' use, so that you don't have to take care of it. And she's going to be right by your side, making sure you get to eat, answering your questions, being your stellar guide.

And she'll also know to keep your difficult family members in check, knowing from her personal relationship with you that peace is important to you. You might not have gotten into that whole thing with your on-site wedding planner. All bases are covered.

Sure, it's an expense to fly in your local wedding planner, and perhaps her assistant, but just one save by your planner can save you thousands of dollars in last-minute rush fees to replace something you're supposed to have at your wedding. Steering a difficult family member away from you all weekend is priceless. The planner's help is worth the cost.

Questions to Ask Your Potential Wedding Planners

For any type of wedding planner, near or far, it's important to ask the right questions while interviewing. You're putting your wedding, and your and your guests' experiences in the hands of this person, so you need to be sure he or she is The One for you. Include these questions in your interview process:

- *What is your accreditation?* A planner will tell you to which associations he or she belongs, a group with strict rules about professionalism, required training and certification, ongoing education and networking. Run from anyone who doesn't have a license or belong to a reputable organization. There are a lot of hobbyists out there who like planning parties and consider themselves to be experts. They may charge far less than true professionals, but you get what you pay for. Expert planners are frustrated by the presence of hobbyists in their midst, but that's nothing compared to the frustration you'll feel when this faux-planner fails you on your wedding day.
- *Have you planned weddings in this destination before?* A planner who has knows the cultural rules and styles that will apply to your wedding.
- *Have you planned weddings at our site before?* It's always a plus when they know the venue inside and out, able to point out a quiet little dining nook for the two of you, or a way to use a balcony, on-site fountains, and additional rooms for your after-party.

Planning Tip

Ask your planner if he or she is familiar with the cultural or religious elements you'd like to include in your day. If not, it may not be a deal-breaker. Planners do a lot of research to plan their weddings well. It's a plus if they are knowledgeable about your choice of cultural or religious wedding wishes.

- *Do you speak the local language for our location?* Always a plus for communication with vendors.
- *What are the details of your wedding planning packages?* And what are the costs for each?
- *Do you charge extra for any services, and what are they?*
- *What is your deposit schedule?*
- *Do you have connections with vendors at our location?* If they do not, ask how they assess the local vendors.
- *What would the timing of our planning process be like?*
- *How accessible will you be?* Some planners are fully accessible, while others will have their assistants handle all of the early work, dealing with you closer to your wedding.
- *Can we communicate via Skype or other online conference sites?* If they answer yes, ask how often they will do so.
- *Can I talk to other couples whose weddings you planned?* If any of their couples married at your wedding location, all the better!
- *Can I see a sample itinerary for a destination wedding you've planned?*
- *Can I see examples of your work?*
- *Will you be willing to travel to our wedding location to work with us there on the wedding weekend?* If the answer is yes, ask what their travel and lodging needs include.
- *What else do we need to know about your work?*

Once you choose your planner, review his or her contract well before signing, and don't be afraid to ask for clarifications. This contract is a legal agreement, to be taken very seriously, because any problems that arise will be handled legally.

Part 2

Planning Your Destination Wedding

AND NOW IT'S time...

Time to plan the details of your wedding, from ceremony to reception to after-party to wedding weekend events for all to enjoy. This is the fun part, your reward for getting through those tough questions including who to invite and how long you have to wait for your big day, who's paying and how much wedding you can afford. Your destination wedding's foundation is set, and now it's time to build on it.

7

Tips for Planning from a Distance

Planning your destination wedding from a distance requires lots of organization and some extra steps to ensure the details and quality you want for your wedding day. You'll have venues and vendors to check out, hire and work with, and you'll face the challenge of not physically being at or near your destination wedding location in order to fulfill each of your tasks in person. It's a lot to deal with. So take these tips to heart, to make the best decisions for the success of your wedding, and to reduce wedding planning stress and extra expense.

- *Set up an excellent organization system.* Decide now if you wish to use online planning tools like budget lists and seating charts on bridal websites, well-rated organizational planning apps like AppyCouple.com or old-school written records to keep track of your venue and vendor searches as well as all of your planning details. Don't take one single step without your organizing system in place.

- *Know your priority lists inside and out.* Talk in depth with each other about what you want for your wedding in its entirety so that you're never thrown into confusion by issues that arise during the planning process. Without any question marks in your wedding vision, you'll be less likely to be swayed into impulse decisions and wasting time and energy. Now this doesn't mean that you won't adjust your vision along the way; it just keeps you in more control of the plans you'll make.

- *Hire a wedding planner.* There's something to be said for a reputable, accredited wedding planner who is local to your wedding destination, who knows your venue or knows the best venues—the same applies to vendors—and likely has planned weddings at your chosen venue in the past. That expert familiarity can save the day when your planner knows about the service at the venue you have your eye on, and has connections to get you the best experts at the best prices. You communicate with your planner, and your planner communicates with the local venue and vendors. This is especially useful when you don't speak the local language very well and your planner does. Communication with every vendor will be key, and your planner will be able to communicate perhaps far better than you can. In addition to language, your local planner may know those unspoken conditions like local vendors who are slow to return messages (because they're on island time), and knows how to navigate those issues best.

- *Schedule a time to visit your venue, or to tour venues, in person.* A little post-engagement scouting trip, even if for just a weekend, revs up your wedding excitement and also allows you to experience each venue, to see how it feels, in order to find The One. Being present at your venue also allows you to sit down for menu and cake tastings, meet with the mixologist to pick out signature drinks, and do all of those fun in-person planning tasks … and to help ensure that you know what you'll actually be getting.

- *Be able to video call with your planner and vendors.* If you don't have video call technology, get it. Face-to-face conversations and negotiations benefit from being able to see body language and facial expressions, hear tone of voice and get a better vibe than you'd get from e-mails or texts in which nuances can be lost and conflict can arise.

- *Have a local point person, if possible.* Let's say you have friends who live in your destination wedding city. If there's something you need done or picked up in-person, your local helper can step in for you. After the wedding, this person gets a thank-you present for their time and efforts on your behalf.
- *Don't be a control freak.* I hear this advice most often from wedding planners and from destination wedding couples. There may be some last-minute changes to your plans, such as your original flower choices not being available due to a freak freeze in their country of origin. When you run into a needed change that is not a deal-breaker (such as your wedding being bumped to a different room in the hotel, something you'd want to fight), keep the bigger picture in mind: you're marrying your best friend and that's going to happen with or without gardenias.
- *Ask your planner and vendors for their preferred method of your sending photos.* You'll need to communicate your vision clearly, and images are the best way to do that. Some vendors don't want to get fifty e-mails of high-resolution photos from you; they'd prefer a Dropbox or Pinterest page for easier image viewing. It's a great question to establish clear communication and consideration for your vendors, one you'd be smart to ask in order to save your own time and energy in sending those pix.
- *Know the time difference where your destination wedding venue and vendors are.* It's a common error to forget about an across-the-ocean time

Destination Wedding Etiquette Tips

Ask your far-away experts for their preferred times for phone calls. Some vendors take calls in the morning, and some at night, so to make your work more efficient and connecting more likely, this is a great question to ask for far-away planning.

zone, calling your planner on her cell at 3:00 a.m., or delaying a time-sensitive booking because their office is closed.

- *Request "view receipts."* Ask for this on all e-mails, so that you know your planner or vendors saw your message.
- *Learn some important phrases in the local language.* It can't hurt to know a few key lines for better communications. At the very least, for an amicable working relationship, learn the greeting and good-bye phrases in your vendors' native language.
- *Understand the local currency.* Use a free currency converter app or website to help you translate the costs you'll face when you're paying on the economy.
- *Return calls right away.* Make a great impression, and don't risk forgetting to call back (which can easily happen when there's a lot of planning and prepping going on).
- *Decide what you'll bring and what you'll buy on-site.* There may be some items you'd prefer to buy at your wedding location, like site-specific wedding favors, so that you won't have to ship them or pay extra baggage fees for a suitcase full of favors. There are probably few items you'll buy on-site, but favors is one that many destination wedding couples opt to get locally, often with their on-site wedding planner's help.
- *Get everything in writing.* Always. Like any wedding, you may have to show an agreement in the vendor's handwriting or via an e-mail to overcome any difference of memories about a conversation or any miscommunications to avoid having to re-configure plans or re-pay a deposit, or have to deal with a lawsuit down the road. Not having things in writing can lead to a lot of stress and heartbreak.

8

Choosing Your Wedding and Reception Venues

ONCE YOU CHOOSE your location, the next step is choosing your ceremony and reception venues. You'll work with your wedding planner to narrow down your options according to your priority list of what you'd like each setting to look and feel like. Images will likely play a big part in this process, so if you haven't already, start pulling some images of gorgeous setting styles into Pinterest boards. The settings don't have to be actual ones from a particular resort. It could be a lodge in Switzerland that can help your planner locate the perfect, similar-looking setting closer to home. You just love the wood beams, the scenery, the lighting, the fireplace. Your planner can then set out to find a short list of venues that provide what you're looking for. So, information/image-gathering is your first step.

The size of your guest list will either open or close possibilities. That sweet little chapel in the Italian countryside would be perfect for your 30 guests, since it holds 40 people. Your 150-person guest list will not work. So think functionality and space for any locations you're looking at. Your venue manager should be able to give you their maximum capacity, which you'll have to honor.

Next, focus more on the feeling and experience your settings will provide. Think about scenery, of course, in the view from the venue and all around it . . . an important factor since the ride or walk to your venue will play a part in setting the scene for your wedding's tone. Here are some experiential factors to consider:

- *Privacy.* Will yours be the only wedding taking place at that venue on your wedding day, or will you be surrounded by other wedding groups taking their photos in those amazing gardens or by that waterfall? If the place is big enough, privacy might not be a factor, but since you'd have to prevent anyone—hotel guest or other stranger—from stepping into your buffet line, what practices does the site enact to keep your event private?
- *A sense of history.* Do you want your venues to tell a story, and immerse your guests in a setting that has a rich sense of ever-present history? Some venues have great "if these walls could talk" stories, such as an Italian village's church where your great-grandparents were married. Or perhaps the estate you're looking at had a rich history of Hollywood legends stopping in to its speakeasy. The history of a place can add further depth to your day.
- *The views.* Does your venue offer a view of the sunset, or colorful trees that will be in full autumn color? Does the rooftop space give you 360-degree views of the city lit up at night?

The settings for your ceremony and reception spot, of course, need to match your dream in appearances. So if you're scouting from a distance, be sure to research many images of the site, from the outside, from the inside, every area of the space that you and your guests will experience. A site could have the most beautiful ballroom you've ever seen, but the building looks run-down from the outside or is located in a not-so-idyllic area. Invest plenty of time to get many views of each location, since your approaches and departures to and from each setting play a big role in your wedding's overall experience.

Planning Tip

Before shopping for your venues, have a detailed list of all of the events you'd like to plan within your wedding weekend. It's easier to scout venues with those events in mind as well, so that you can book the perfect, multi-setting location.

The next factor to consider is how many spaces at each setting you'll get to use—again, the privacy factor—expanded to get you thinking about all of the events you'd like to plan. For instance, does the resort have a great open-air terrace for a welcome cocktail party? Would you be able to plan your cocktail party poolside? Would the resort rope off their pool at 6:00 p.m. for your private event? Is there a bar on the premises where your after-party could occur, or a separate, smaller party room for that VIP party?

Now think more deeply about timing. If you'd like a sunset wedding ceremony on the beach, that could mean your reception would be shorter, considering the resort's 10:00 p.m. noise curfew, the time when they shut down receptions as a rule. Day versus night venue appearances can vary tremendously, and can impact your budget. For instance, an afternoon ceremony on the beach, followed by a reception ending at sunset, means that nature will be your lighting expert. A nighttime ceremony and reception calls for much more detailed lighting effects that will have to be designed and brought in to illuminate your settings. And, to you, how does a daytime wedding feel versus a nighttime wedding? You may have had different experiences in day or night weddings you've attended, so if you know that nighttime is the right time for your destination wedding, then your venue search will take on different locations on your short list depending on how they look and feel in the evening.

As you and your wedding planner are searching for your venues, you're going to bump into the sites' rules and regulations, which may qualify or negate sites. For instance, some places will not allow tents to be installed on their property, to protect their grounds. So your dream of a tented outdoor wedding would come into play as a deal-breaker for those sites. Some sites have certain dates or times when they will not allow weddings, and some sites don't allow weddings at all. Your wedding planner will know what your wedding dream requires, so he or she will know which questions to ask at the outset, such as whether or not you can set up the tent the caterer needs specifically for food prep and plating. Some locations, like churches, will not allow flash photography. And some will not allow your floral designer to create floral décor pieces on-site. They would have to build them off-site and ferry them in or drive them in already constructed. It's all of these rules you may not expect that can play a big part in choosing your venues.

And speaking of rules, some sites will not allow you to bring in outside vendors. You would have to work with their on-site or preferred vendors. (This might not be a problem for you. You might see this as making everything easier, provided their vendors are good professionals. You'll have to research them.) And ask about other regulations. Don't make assumptions, especially for a destination wedding in another culture. Get their lists, and make sure you adhere to them.

Some other considerations:

• *Ask how many items you will have to rent.* In order to hold your ceremony or reception at this location, you may need to furnish specific items. Some places have tables and chairs already, and some don't. Some places have linens, silverware, serving tables, and so on. And other places don't. So think about the impact on your budget that a long list of rentals would make.

- *Ask if you can change their décor.* Some places have artwork on the walls that you won't be allowed to take down to replace with your own décor for the day. Some places will remove their furniture to make room for the décor you want, and other places won't let you move anything to protect their flooring.

- *Ask if you can speak to other couples who have married there.* And ask specifically for couples who have held weddings similar in size and scope to your wedding. If the spokesperson says he or she can't provide any references, move on. The site should be able to show you some photos from these couples' weddings, but it's always preferable to talk to the couple themselves.

- *Ask if you can make any substitutions in their wedding package.* You might not want a wedding cake, preferring a dessert bar instead, so can you have the cost of a cake removed from your package and adjusted for the cost of the dessert bar? Is their package set in stone, or are there any other customizations you can make? Some places won't budge on their wedding package, since they whip out identical weddings with just some colors and floral types differing from their norm. And compare what's in each venue's packages to get a better sense of cost comparisons between places.

- *Ask about price differences.* Depending upon the season, date, or time of day, there may be room for negotiation.

- *Ask about room layouts and dimensions.* Make sure you can design your wedding events the way you'd like, and also have plenty of room for your number of guests.

- *Ask about parking.* Is there a free lot, or will guests need to find for-pay parking elsewhere or pay to park in the hotel's lot or garage?

- *Ask about deposit amounts and schedules.*

- *Ask to see a copy of their contract in advance.* Ask the staff for time to review your contract before signing. There will be many details and rules in any agreement, and you'll want to read yours carefully—and have your planner read it carefully as well—in order to be sure you're agreeing to all the right things and not missing anything potentially tragic in the contract.

- *Ask about transportation.* Can you arrange transportation by the resort, hopefully for free, between the ceremony and reception for all of your guests? If not, how do most wedding couples arrange transportation for their guests?
- *Ask if children are allowed.* Some resorts are adults-only, and some welcome families during certain times of the year.
- *Ask about accessibility if you have any mobility-challenged guests.* Some venues will provide, or have, ramps and personal rides to and from your settings.
- *Ask about site fees.* Some locations charge fees for use of their beaches, bluffs, rooftop settings, and other spaces, on top of wedding costs. An in-demand beach with the best views may cost several thousand dollars more than booking a smaller, yet pretty beach on the other side of the resort.
- *Ask about lodging.* Are there enough rooms on-site to lodge your guests, or will this venue be able to suggest other nearby hotels for some of your guests to use? Take a look at the rooms online or on a site visit to help with your decision about the right home for your guests.
- *Ask about any future plans for renovations.* You don't want your wedding hotel to be a construction zone, with scaffolding and noise everywhere. If the venue has plans for room remodels, will they be done way before your wedding? Keep in mind for this question that any kind of remodeling or refurbishment can always take longer than expected. You might opt, for peace of mind, to avoid any venue that has a fix-up on the horizon, or take your chances and book if you're feeling lucky. But it's a smart question to ask.
- *Ask if you can do a tasting.* Some places hold this as a standard for your site visit, and other places do not. So can you dine at the restaurant or

hotel to get a taste of their cuisine? Some sites will let you meet with their caterer or chef to customize your menu, even going off of their set wedding menu. Ask about personalizing your menus.

- *Ask if someone on their staff can help you plan.* If you wish to add additional fun during the wedding weekend/week, ask if there is a staff member who can coordinate activities and whether there is a wedding group discount should your guests want to participate.
- *Ask if the site will have any existing decorations.* Ask if the venue will be "bare bones" for you to decorate. Some sites maintain their own floral décor and other accents that may be perfectly fine for your event.

We've been focusing on hotels and your reception for the most part here, so let's turn to your ceremony site for a minute. Ask about their rules for your permission to marry there. Will you have to prove that you are a practicing member of their faith? Will they allow interfaith weddings? What will you have to pay for? Some places require a fee for their officiant, a fee for their cleanup person, musician, and other staffers. And some charge a fee to have photos taken on their premises. Be sure you're getting their rules as well, since many houses of worship have long lists of instructions. And again, never make assumptions. Just because your house of worship back home does weddings a certain way doesn't mean a house of worship in the same denomination overseas or in any other town will do things the same way.

Don't Forget

For a beach wedding, ask if that beach is for private use of the hotel's guests, or if it can be booked to be private for your event . . . or will the place be crowded with tourists all around you? Some sites will charge a site fee for blocking off your beach for your event.

If you can't go on a scouting trip before you need to book venues, you'll need to go by images of the sites. Which can be a challenge, since you never know how old their photos are. So do a lot of research online, checking all of their social media sites, as well as scanning the Internet for Real Weddings held at that setting. Check Vimeo and YouTube as well for video highlights from weddings that took place there, and Instagram will also have tagged photos and videos taken at your locations.

If you can go on a scouting trip before you book, arrange your schedule to get you in those doors as early in your stay as possible, in case you don't like something about a venue and will then have time to go looking at some new ones.

Once you have your ceremony and reception venues booked, you can look for the perfect venues for your welcome cocktail party, rehearsal dinner, breakfast, and after-party, plus settings for any wedding weekend events you'll host, using the same advice you found here about the venue's size and functionality as well as its feel. Here are some additional considerations for these other events that will become part of your destination wedding experience:

- *Look at venues that offer a different view from your wedding settings.* For instance, if your reception will be held indoors, perhaps your welcome cocktail party can be held on the beach. If you love different things about your location, these additional events let you and your guests experience these wonderful other glimpses of the setting. If your wedding will be in a big city ballroom, for instance, your welcome cocktail party can be held at a rooftop bar with a grand view. If your island wedding will be on land, your rehearsal dinner can be held aboard a yacht. Think indoor versus outdoor, and all of the sights you'd like to serve as backdrop for any of your events.
- *Look at venues that offer a different type of menu from your wedding.* You may have chosen a classic wedding menu with filet mignon and lobster, and for your rehearsal dinner, you can choose a menu featuring more of your location's cultural dishes, such as jambalaya or a wider range of island seafood dishes.

- *Mix up the formality.* If your wedding will be formal, plan an informal welcome party on the beach, with guests sitting on blankets and pillows on the sand before low-set tables, in casual attire and in bare feet. Remember that guests' comfort level is key to a great destination wedding, so when you provide a range of formality levels and styles, you'll hit upon more guests' favorite celebration types.
- *Limit the lengths of your wedding weekend events.* Aim to keep open bar costs down. Plus, shorter "must attend" events allow guests more downtime and free time for their own gatherings and relaxation.
- *Don't worry too much about décor at these other events.* Going minimal lets your wedding décor stand out and drop jaws in comparison.
- *Plan unique signature drinks at each of these events.* Even if it's just giving a mimosa a new name. That gives you more creative fun in your planning and adds a little something extra to these parties.
- *Incorporate your other choices.* Couldn't decide on one favorite cake flavor for your wedding? Use your second choice for a cake served at your rehearsal dinner. In fact, many of your second-choice and third-choice ideas can be "recycled" for inclusion in these events, letting you have many more of your favorite wedding ideas throughout your stay. And if you'll have a post-wedding party back home, even more of your ideas can come into play.
- *Coordinate wedding week/weekend event locations.* If someone else wants to host a breakfast or dinner for you, make sure you have a say in picking the location. You don't want them to "scoop" your rehearsal dinner spot with their own dinner event prior to yours, or take the last available booking. Explain to your wonderful, giving friend or relative that you need to coordinate all of your events and will be happy to recommend locations in that area. Add in the benefit of having your wedding planner available for referrals and inside scoop on the restaurants, for the event's ultimate success. Your host will likely be relieved not to have to site-shop from a distance and can focus on the fun stuff like décor and menu selections.

- *Remain flexible.* As with your entire wedding, you'll need to be flexible and accept that some changes may need to happen with your plans. Anything from market pricing to a shortage of oysters to some other huge event at your location scooping up all the lilies can require shifts in your plans. Keep the bigger picture in mind and just enjoy the clams and peonies.

9

Choosing Your Vendors

ONCE YOU HAVE your locations picked out and booked, you can start the research process of finding the perfect vendors, those wedding professionals who can enhance your wedding vision with their own suggestions and handle the many complicated steps of bringing your vision to life. They'll bring their A-game not only to your wedding, but also to the entire process of working with you along the way. Your wedding is in their hands. The food is going to depend on the people making it. Your bouquet is going to depend on the person making it. The band gets the energy up and keeps the dance floor packed. You want experienced, high-quality professionals who will make your events unforgettable.

Finding Vendors

Now if your wedding will be at an all-inclusive or a resort with a full wedding package including the cake, catering, photographer, and entertainment, you won't have to deal with finding and hiring the best professionals in the area. Your chosen resort has brought the quality to your party, including professionals they know and respect who make them shine as well with their fabulous service. Does this mean you won't have to talk to those professionals? Not at all. You'll still get to meet with them, either virtually or in person, and work on details with them. You just won't have to sift through hundreds of wedding vendors to find the right ones first.

If you do need to find the perfect professionals for your destination wedding, keep in mind that you won't necessarily only be working with local talent. At more and more destination weddings, couples are flying in their wedding planner and photographer, sometimes their beauty experts and other professionals to have them work the wedding on-site. The advantages of working with local-to-you vendors prior to the wedding are many. You'll get to meet in person and work on details together in person, and if your wedding location creates a language barrier when you don't speak the native tongue and it's been tough to find local vendors who do, it could be smart to work with a local-to-you expert. And think about how you'll need to work with your photographer and videographer after the wedding, ordering prints and albums. It can be far easier to work with a local vendor on this task than with someone who is located far away.

On the flip side, a vendor who is located at your destination may have done weddings at your venues before, knowing their inner workings and the issues they know to address with the management. They may know best what is needed to rent for an outside wedding at your site, which privacy steps to take in surprising

Planning Tip

Keep in mind the whole idea of "island time," which doesn't just apply to islands. While you may be used to rapid-fire responses to e-mails and texts, the local speed of reply may be much slower. It's just part of the culture, and not always a reflection of professionalism on behalf of the vendor you're waiting to hear back from.

areas of the resort, which questions to ask. And they can clue you in to other local vendors you should consider. Familiarity is an advantage. As is fluency in the local language and in the culture's ways of doing business.

To begin your process of finding excellent vendors—true professionals who will amaze you with their talent—set up a time to talk with your wedding planner. He or she may have a terrific list of personal contacts, and can also check around with their reputable sources to find local talent for you. Ones that come highly recommended. That's your step one.

Step two is talking with couples who married at your actual venue, or in the region where your venue is located. They will be able to share their research, including who they hired and loved, who they hired and wished they didn't, who they passed up, and who they wished they hadn't passed up. They may have interviewed the perfect floral designer at their wedding's location, but she was booked on their wedding day. With their recommendation, you might be able to snag her for your day. Make this process smoother by asking specifically about types of vendors. If you just ask, "Who did you hire?" you might just get a few names off the tops of their heads. If you're more specific, asking about photographers, videographers, bakers, and such, you may get more valuable input.

I also like to advise checking with friends and family who attended a wedding at your location, or close to it. They can tell you if the food was divine, the band

Planning Tip

Look also at Real Wedding features on wedding blogs and in wedding magazines. When your online scouting turns up a wedding that takes your breath away, located at or near your wedding venue, the vendors' names and URLs will be right there in the story. And many of the top wedding blogs and magazines feature their favorite vendors, who may be featured on the website multiple times. Don't forget to search their company name on that site to turn up all of the weddings the website has featured.

excellent, the décor impressive. If they loved anything about the wedding they went to, they can potentially ask their friend the bride for the name of that amazing caterer or band. Most people are all too happy to help, *but* you have to make sure the person you're checking with will ultimately be on your wedding guest list. You don't want anyone to help you plan your wedding and then not get an invite . . . or think they will be getting an invite. It's a sticky etiquette thing to pay attention to. Because people make assumptions when you ask them to help with your wedding plans. So stick with your close circle of friends, family, and bridal party members for these referrals, just to be on the safe side.

Read reviews of your vendors on multiple sites, and pay special attention to their own websites. That's where you'll find their lists of the professional associations to which they belong, any awards they've won, their additional social media platforms, lists of where they have worked, and especially links to their blogs. While many vendors hire professional writers to create their content, some write their own blog posts, giving you a sense of their personalities and what they love about their jobs. It's just another in a string of research steps to take. I like to look at vendors' Instagram posts, to see videos of them in action, dazzling photos of their work, and inspiring memes that give you a glimpse of their philosophies. The more you can scout out about any vendor, including those your venue requires as part of their wedding package, the more you know about how you may be able to connect.

When to Start Looking for Vendors

Start looking for vendors as soon as possible, perhaps right now if you haven't begun, since the best wedding experts in any popular destination wedding location can get booked up way in advance. Many couples forget that destination wedding professionals are also doing local weddings, and in peak season they may book up more than a year in advance. I've seen some top wedding planners in popular destination wedding locations booked for three years in advance. So don't delay. You want the best of the best working for you.

How Do We Do All of This Interviewing from Far Away?

If you can't take a scouting trip right now, to book your vendors and maybe your venues as well, then you have several options. One is to have your wedding planner—local to your wedding's site—meet with potential vendors, and send you his or her notes on each candidate in order to narrow down your options or get right to picking The One in each category. Your local-to-you wedding planner can also get on the phone and on Skype to pre-interview candidates at your destination wedding location, again sending you his or her notes on each. Together, you'll work toward finding the ideal candidates for their talent, availability, price, and vibe, and look closely at their contracts and agreements before signing on the dotted line. This is an important step, since your wedding planner knows all of the contract language that should be expected in a contract, as well as any hidden language that should be changed or eliminated. A great planner will find all of the hidden fees as well.

At this point, you might wish to Skype with your top two or three vendors, to get your own feel for the experts and what they do.

Not everything is on a vendor's website, so when you reach out to your contenders, ask them for any links to samples of their work, plus any documents they have with their menus, package details, and additional information. Ask also for

Planning Tip

How could it be possible that a vendor isn't online? It actually is possible that talented professionals don't have a website or social media platform, depending upon where they're located and their chosen work methods. Some performers might not want to be bothered with Web hosting and with keeping up with a blog. They just play their guitar, their steel pan, or other instrument, and they're excellent at it. They may have an e-mail but no website, so if you'd like to interview them, you can ask them to e-mail or mail you samples of their work, or let you know where video of their work may be shown online.

references, and here is your script for contacting these couples who have worked in the past with this vendor:

> Hello, (reference's name)!
>
> (Vendor's name), your wedding (vendor's job), provided me with your e-mail address so that I may ask for your insights about the work (he/she) did for your wedding. Were you pleased with (his/her) work for your wedding? What did you like about (his/her) work, and do you have any thoughts about this vendor's weaknesses or challenges? Would you recommend them to your family and friends? Thank you in advance for your time and assistance. I appreciate your taking the time to help us out as we plan our wedding.
>
> > Have a great day,
> > (Your name)
> > (Your e-mail address)

Since you're writing to a stranger, keep in mind that your e-mail may go to their spam file, but hopefully your message will get through to them, and that they're the type of people to get right back to you. When a couple loves their vendors, they want to help them out in return for the excellent service they provided, so these couples who likely told their vendor they'd be happy to be references will have useful information to share.

What to Get in Writing

The vendors you speak with will be interviewing you as well, to find out your wishes for your wedding, the scope and size of your wedding, the formality and all of the details you have in mind so far. Vendors will then figure out all they'll need to do, how much time it will take, how many assistants they will need, and what costs will be, and they'll prepare an official proposal for your review. As well as your wedding planner's review.

The proposal will contain the following:

- Your wedding date
- Your wedding location(s)
- Their travel requirements and fees
- The number of hours they will be performing or working for your wedding
- Exact items in your order, right down to the number of white roses in your floral order, the model number of the silverware you like and how many pieces that will need to be rented, menu details such as serving style and any particular menu package, and so on
- Their fees
- Their overtime fees
- Deposit amounts and deadlines, plus method of payment
- Cancellation policy
- Other details

You'll review the proposal and communicate with your wedding planner about any questions that need to be asked or issues that need to be clarified before you do any official hiring.

This will happen for each of your vendors. Your wedding planner is going to be crucial to this process, since they may have to follow up with vendors who haven't yet sent a proposal, communicate with vendors about their proposals, and use their skills to negotiate with the vendors. There is almost always room for negotiation, no matter the size of your wedding. Don't think that vendors won't want your small wedding, and won't be willing to throw in some extras or make substitutions. Every good vendor knows that you are connected to a world of friends and family, and your referral or online reviews can connect them to additional event bookings. So don't apologize for your small wedding, and don't shy away from negotiating. Your planner can take the reins here, if you're worried about a vendor considering you to be a "difficult" client. They know how to negotiate smoothly and professionally, reviewing multiple proposals and negotiating with your finalists on your behalf.

Contract Time

Once you decide on your vendors, you'll receive from each a contract, which you'll review with your wedding planner before signing. Again, contracts have important, specific language in them that can help deliver the best service, and determine also what you'll have to deal with if you need to cancel or challenge the contract in court. Which I hope you'll never have to do. A fine-tooth comb review of all contracts can help save you from that nightmare. Contracts are binding agreements, so pay special attention to yours.

Each contract should include the following:

- The company name, street address, phone number, and e-mail
- The name of the person responsible for your event
- The date of your wedding
- The time of your wedding
- The location(s) of your wedding
- A complete description of your product or service, right down to the flavors of the cake, to the types of musicians in the band, the number of bouquets and the types of flowers in them, and so on
- Exact start and finish times for your event, including setup and cleanup, to specify what counts as working time, and what counts as overtime
- Overtime rules and fees
- Travel times and fees, if applicable
- Exact prices, including tips and service charges, taxes, payment method, deposit schedule, payment deadlines, late fees, and all other charges
- Insurance information for the vendor
- Dress code for the staff or vendor
- Cancellation/refund/rescheduling policy and fees
- Cleanup and return of rentals details
- After-wedding responsibilities and delivery dates, such as delivery of albums and video

Talk to your wedding planner about any language you don't understand in your contract. (Yes, even though your wedding planner will review the contract, you should look it over closely as well.) Multiple sets of eyes can be a bonus in spotting anything vague or incomplete. Some couples spotted the wrong wedding date or location in their contract, getting it fixed in time. Don't worry about asking a dumb question. Wedding planners have heard everything, and they like to work with conscientious, focused, detail-oriented couples. Your questions help them work more smoothly with you, avoiding any assumptions or unwelcome surprises.

And it goes without saying that you should never hire or work with a vendor who doesn't offer a contract. That has nightmare written all over it.

Okay, now that we've gone over the business end of choosing and hiring vendors, let's get into specifics of each type of vendor you'll hire. Keep these questions in front of you as you do your interviewing.

Caterers

They say that the food makes the wedding, and they're so right. A delectable menu at every stage of your wedding, from welcome cocktail party to your wedding morning breakfast, rehearsal dinner, cocktail party, reception, after-party, and morning-after breakfast is key to everyone's enjoyment. So with this long list of destination wedding events, you may have more than one catering company involved, unless you choose to have your resort cater each of your events.

Here are your questions to ask:

- *Do you offer set menus in each of your packages?* Or will we get to choose the individual dishes? Never assume that caterers operate like weddings you've been to at home. Some have one menu for a cocktail party wedding, with few variations. Most will have different levels of catering packages, offering a greater number of hors d'oeuvres in the cocktail party, and more or different courses in higher-priced packages.

- *Can you help us pick out menu items for each of our events?* A chef's refined palate can be a benefit to your wedding events, with his or her expertise in mixing up dishes taking your menus to a new level.
- *Do you offer specialty dishes?* Discuss such items as vegan, gluten-free, vegetarian, Paleo, kosher, and so on, depending on your guests' dietary needs.
- *How do you handle food allergies for our guests?* Do you set out ID cards for each dish on the cocktail party buffet, letting guests know which dishes have nuts, etc.?
- *Can you recommend any local or specialty dishes?* Ask if there are seasonal items or cultural dishes that will enhance the menu.
- *Can we make changes to a particular package?* Can we add a few more hors d'oeuvres or eliminate a dinner course we don't want?
- *Do you offer any kid-friendly dishes?* Are there other selections for your child guests to choose from?
- *Does all the food need to be made by you?* Can we bring in some dishes from another local source? Your caterer might not allow, say, a food truck outside their venue.
- *Can we make changes later to take advantage of market prices for meats and seafood?* Caterers must buy the food for your wedding, of course, and may be able to tell you that a particular kind of meat or seafood is better priced than what you originally wanted, or that a certain type of seafood is not plentiful on the market right now. If you're flexible and open to your caterer's better picks, it may work to your budget's benefit.
- *What is the best serving style for our cocktail party and dinner?* Passed hors d'oeuvres may be better for certain types of foods that need to be served hot, while other dishes do better on a buffet line. And you'll need to decide if you like family-style service at guests' tables, or if you'd like their dishes individually plated and served.
- *Do you offer upgrades?* Are there specialty stations that we can add to our event?
- *Do you offer the wedding cake and desserts?*

- *Will stations be manned by servers?* If not, will platters be set out for guests' self-service?
- *How many servers will be circulating with hand-passed trays?* How many servers will you have on site overall?
- *What do the servers wear?* You'd likely want them to match the formality of your event.
- *Can we arrange for a tasting of menu options to help us decide?* Some venues do not do tastings, so make sure you know what to expect, including how many people can attend the tasting. You may wish to bring along bridal party members or parents if your location is close enough for them to realistically travel to with you during your scouting trips.
- *What types of linens, place settings, tables, and chairs are available for our wedding?* You might have wishes for Chivari chairs or long tables with benches, so you'll need to make sure your venue can comply, or that you can rent and bring in the table styles and other details you want.
- *What are the fees?* Ask the vendor to provide the fee amount for each element of your wedding, including room setup, bartenders, carving station attendants, and more—expenses outside of the per-guest fees for food, dessert, and drinks.
- *Is there a corkage or pouring fee?* Some venues charge a nominal amount for each bottle of wine or champagne their bartenders will open. Make sure you know what the corkage fees are, since they can be lofty at some venues. Ask as well if corkage fees only apply to liquor you bring in from an outside source.
- *Is there a cake-cutting fee?* Some venues will charge you a few dollars per slice of wedding cake that has to be cut and plated during your reception. Ask if there is a cake-cutting fee for the cake that's included in your wedding package, and if there is a cake-cutting fee only for a cake you bring in from an outside baker.
- *What is your deposit schedule?*
- *When is the deadline for final guest headcount?*
- *What is your policy for non-attenders?* If we get last-minute cancellations, do you have a policy of not charging for no-shows?

- *Do you offer vendor meals?* Many venues will prepare cheaper dinner dishes for your photographer, band, and other on-site vendors. If you have many cancellations, can you arrange for your vendors to be given those guests' pricier meals instead?
- *Is a champagne toast included?* Many all-inclusive packages will include a round of champagne pours, and you'll have to check to see if your venue provides for this. If not, you may need to talk to your bar manager about your champagne wishes.
- *How are tips and service charges arranged and distributed?*
- *How many weddings are you working that weekend?* Ask how many weddings the caterer usually works on a weekend, to gauge the kind of attention your wedding will receive.
- *Will you require any tents or additional equipment to work at our wedding location?* Some caterers require their own tents where they will prep, plate, and garnish dishes, shielding them from your guests' view at the wedding.
- *Will you need to look at the kitchen where we will hold our event?* Some independent caterers will need to make sure their platters will fit into the refrigerator or oven on-site, and check power sources and power supply. They may need to bring in their own refrigerators and generator if the place is not up to their standards.
- *Have you worked at our venue before?* An independent caterer who knows that kitchen is a benefit.
- *Do you have any requests for me?* Ask the caterer what questions he or she has for you as well . . .

Cake Baker and Dessert Chef

Just like with your caterer, you may have multiple events at which you'd like to have cakes, so you may be questioning for different events, or possibly interviewing multiple cake bakers and dessert chefs. The tastes of these creations is also paramount for the success of your wedding, since a dry, taste-free, or too sweet cake can wreck your wedding right at the end. You'll want to be sure these sweet treats and fruity bites will be pleasing to all, and that your cakes and desserts will be gorgeous. So here are some of the most important questions to ask your dessert bakers:

+ *What are your most popular cake styles?* Some all-inclusives and resorts offer one type of cake: a three-tiered cake with round layers. And some offer a range of cake shapes, sizes, and styles. Independent bakers, if you're allowed to use them at your venue, will likely offer a range of cake options.
+ *What are the cake flavors, fillings, and frostings we can choose from?* You'll be shown their list of standard flavors, as well as flavors in their premium selections for extra cost. Many cake bakers create lists of their premium flavors, since they will go to a farmer's market to get organic fruit for the filling, and some types of fillings and frostings simply cost more due to their ingredients.
+ *Do you make our favorite type of cake?* Personalized weddings can call for custom choices, such as a rum cake or carrot cake—your favorites. Does the cake baker at your location know how to make these types of cakes, and is their version of a carrot cake similar to what you know to be a carrot cake? They may make them differently in your location, so ask about ingredients.
+ *Can we get a gluten-free cake, or make changes to account for any food allergies?* You'll have to make sure there are no nuts in the cake if a guest or you have allergies, and that you know about other ingredients that can be unexpected or problematic.
+ *Are there any kinds of local cake flavors or fillings that we can consider to work our location and its culture into our wedding day?* There may be a traditional kind of wedding cake for your location that you'd like to include, as a whole cake or as one of your cake's layers or groom's cake.
+ *Can we get a groom's cake as well?* For the groom's cake, which flavors can we consider?
+ *What are your cake décor styles?* Some locations' bakers are not familiar with making sugar paste flowers or those frosting ruffles you've seen on

Instagram. Bakers take courses to learn those methods, and some expert bakers around the world may not be familiar with those styles. So stick with what they do know how to do well, rather than challenging them to learn a new style and possibly not do it as well as you'd like.

- *Are there any heights of cake that you will not transport?* Some bakers will be happy to truck a three-tiered cake to your location, but a seven-tiered cake is just too much work, requiring too much manpower and risk.
- *What is your delivery system?* You'll need to make sure your baker has a contact person available at your venue while you're getting ready for your wedding. And that your baker knows how you'd like your cake to be displayed. Ask if there is a delivery fee as well.
- *Do you offer more than the wedding cake?* Which other kinds of desserts do you make that we can add to our dessert hour?
- *Will we be allowed to bring in desserts from another baker?* You might discover a specialty dessert baker whose treats you wish to bring in. Your venue might have a rule about no outside desserts, so know this rule before you order and put down a deposit.
- *Have you worked at our venue before?* They won't bake the cake there, but if there are a lot of stairs leading to your venue, or other space issues, that's important to know.
- *Will you work with our floral designer to coordinate cake flowers with our décor flowers?* Your baker may be able to make sugar-paste or buttercream versions of flowers, or suggest edible flowers to put on your cake.
- *When do you make the cake?* You want a fresh cake, not one that's been made a week prior and frozen. You will all be able to taste freezer burn, so be sure you're getting a fresh cake.
- *How can we have the cake displayed?* Can we put mini-desserts around the base?
- *How do you make sure the cake is illuminated?* Will you work with the venue's lighting specialist to be sure the cake is lit well?

- *Can we get a cake topper from you?*
- *Can we get a cake knife and serving knife from you?* Your venue may supply these, but you might want your own set to take home for your anniversary cake cutting and serving.
- *Do you have any advice for us?* Some bakers will suggest not keeping your cake out on display due to your location's heat and humidity levels. The cake will be much safer from melting and collapsing if it's kept in a refrigerator and wheeled out for cutting. And some locations have mosquitoes, gnats, and flies that are attracted to the sweet frosting, dotting the cake with their carcasses and grossing out your guests.
- *What is your policy for the cake that remains after it is served?* Will we be able to take a piece of cake back to our room after the reception, or bring leftover cake to the after-party?
- *What is your deposit schedule?*
- *What are your tipping and service charge policies?*
- *What is your cancellation policy?*
- *What happens if we wish to change our cake design or flavors?* Is there a date by which we can make any changes without added fees? Is there a fee for changing our cake or dessert order?

Floral Designer

Your floral designer's talented eye for details brings the magic of your wedding décor to life, and sets in your hand a gorgeous bouquet to complete your bridal look. Floral designers may also transform your setting with candlelight and lanterns, illuminating your space to make it truly breathtaking. It's artistry at its finest, springing from a gifted knowing of which kinds of flowers will do best in the climate as well as how to group flora and foliage to best effect. If one of your top priorities is your flowers and décor, this vendor will have to be spectacular.

To help you select the best floral designer for you, provided you're not in an all-inclusive resort package situation that dictates who your floral designer will be—yet, again, important to interview them at the start of your process—here are some important questions to ask:

- *How would you like to receive images of floral arrangements and bouquets that I love?* Some vendors prefer to look at a Pinterest page, and some like Dropbox sends, not wanting you to jam up their computer with e-mails of high-resolution images. Ask this important question at the outset, and your floral designer will love you for your consideration.
- *What are some local flowers and greenery that we can incorporate into our floral designs?* You may not know much about local flowers, but they do. And some venues have gardens from which they cut their florals and greenery for budget breaks.
- *Can I get a list of which flowers and greenery are in-season at the time of our wedding?*
- *If our chosen flowers aren't available on the wedding day, which types of flowers will you substitute?*
- *Can you recommend any flowers that have scent—or no scent—to fulfill our wishes for sensory detailing?* Some people love for the room to smell like gardenias, and other people are sensitive to too much scent. Ask your floral designer to strike the perfect balance.
- *Are there any flowers that you especially love working with?* Any floral combinations that you really love and can recommend?
- *Are there any local customs and traditions related to wedding flowers and greenery?* If your location has a "good luck" wedding flower, you'll surely want it to be part of your day.
- *Have you worked at our venue before?* Your floral designer may already know about a great part of your venue to festoon with flowers, banisters to decorate, and the perfect place for a floral wall or arch. They may know about a low ceiling or other challenge, and have already overcome it at

other weddings, and if they haven't worked a wedding at your venue before, arrange for them to take a visit for a scouting trip of their own, perhaps joining you on your scouting trip.

- *Will you be involved with the floral design setup at our location?* Some floral designers get all of the flowers together, then send them to the venue for workers there to set up. You will likely want the person you've been communicating with to be on-site, arranging flowers just the way you like.
- *Are there any floral accents you recommend for our site?* Your designer may know that the wooden bridge to your ceremony site can use a garland or florals.
- *If we can come in for a pre-wedding meeting, can we arrange to see samples of our wedding floral designs?* A floral designer might not be able to make versions of your bouquets and centerpieces if that's not the norm for their culture, but it can't hurt to ask. You may be able to view what they're working on at the time, though.
- *Can we arrange to have our wedding florals and bouquets donated to any local nursing homes or hospitals after the wedding?*
- *Do you have any other décor items available for rent or use?* Many floral designers have on hand décor pieces they used at another wedding, then re-use for other events. Sometimes these items are available for free. Ask about pedestals and other display items as well as actual décor pieces.
- *What is the latest date when we can make any changes or additions to our floral order?*

Budget Tip

If there are pricey flowers in the images you send to your floral designer, ask if there are any local, lower-cost, similar flowers than can be used beautifully in your designs.

- *What is your deposit schedule?*
- *What is your cancellation policy?*
- *What are your terms for service charges and tips?*

Photographer and Videographer

Again, you may choose to hire and fly in your photography and videography experts, since there are many tasks to work on with them months after your wedding. It can be difficult to reach, coordinate with, and remedy any problems with photo and video professionals way back at your destination wedding location, making fixes or refunds difficult or impossible. So if you do decide to bring in your own local photographer and videographer, the interviewing phase can be easier when they're a town or two away from you. Some couples, valuing their photos over their video, choose to fly in their photographer and use a local videographer.

Here are some important questions to ask when interviewing and hiring your photo and video pros:

- *Do you belong to any professional associations?* Photo and video pros may be members of accredited associations that provide ongoing education, new technology workshops, and conferences at which these pros continue to advance their craft. To be in these associations, they have to have good records of service, and be true professionals, not hobbyists who own a great camera and shoot weddings as a way to make some extra money. You'll want high professional standards in your photo and video pros.
- *Do you shoot in photojournalistic style?* This style of wedding photography captures natural moments as they occur, telling the story of your day, instead of posed group shots and portrait style. For instance, a photojournalistic style can capture the interactions at a guest table, whereas a posed group shot can look like those table shots from the prom. Look through lots of samples of the photographer's work to check out their style of

shooting. You'll get a feel for their shooting philosophy and also discover some shots that you'll definitely want added to your own shots' list.

- *Can we see samples of your work?* In addition to the samples, galleries, and videos you'll see on their websites, your pros will also have additional albums, slideshows, and videos that you may see for the asking. Ask to see actual albums, to get a feel for how your albums will look and feel, as opposed to online slideshows. For your videographer, ask to see a wedding video, not just a highlight reel, to get a good idea of how your full wedding video will look as well. And then ask to see a highlight video, to get a feel for how your highlight reel will look and sound.

- *When will we be able to see proofs?* If you hire someone local to you, the timetable may not be a big issue for you. Proofs might take weeks or months to come in, which is close to the norm. Edited photos will take longer. If you hire a photo or video professional located at your destination wedding region, ask about time for processing and delivery before you leave, and of course have this detail written in your contract.

- *Will you bring along assistants?* There may be extra charges for assistants, and you'll also want to be sure they're included in your headcount list at your venue so that they have a seat and vendor meals available for them. Ask how the assistants will be used on the wedding day, as well. Some will carry equipment and some will be "second shooters" or "third shooters," capturing your ceremony and other big moments from several different angles at the same time.

- *What kind of equipment do you use, and which format do you shoot in?* You may not know much about photo and video equipment, but your professionals' explanations can be illuminating. It's important that they have new and elite equipment, and that the format they shoot in will deliver the best quality photos and footage. You may have heard about the debate between shooting on film and shooting digitally. You'll be able to see the difference in detail and color when you ask your photographer to show you samples, if possible. Take a look at the crispness and color saturation of black-and-white photos as well, which provides you with a lot of clarity in image contrast, and will also show you how your own black-and-white photos will look. Digital images can, of course, be transformed into sepia or black-and-white, so look at these color tones for your own consideration. For video, most footage will be shot in digital format, but do ask to see differences in color edits for black-and-white footage as well.

- *Can we see samples of your albums?* When you're in the same room with your photographer, you can see and hold their sample albums, getting a feel for their leather-bound or linen-bound albums for your orders. Ask also for the pricing of any additional albums you wish to order. Some packages will provide one main album for the two of you, and if you want to get professional albums for your parents, that's an extra order added on to your package.

- *How long will it take to get albums?* Even without a deadline, it's important to know what you can expect, and plan your follow-up calls, if needed.

- *Can we submit a list of must-get photos?* Most photo and video pros welcome your wish list, and honor it. Some photo and video professionals will have checklists of their own for you to fill out, so that they and their assistants know which shots to get.

- *Have you ever shot a wedding at our location before?* If so, they may know the perfect scenic setting, taking advantage of the perfect lighting during the day or evening, to get great shots and footage. If not, or if you're bringing in your own professional who has never been to your destination wedding location, ask if they have ever shot your type of wedding before. You'll want a photo and video pro who knows what's involved in shooting on a beach, or in cooler weather, or on a yacht.

- *Will you be available to meet us at our wedding venue prior to the wedding day for a brief tour?* Together, you can scout out great places to take your photos and video segments.

Planning Tip

Assign a friend to help the photographer in IDing any special relatives or families you'd like them to photograph. They don't have to tail them all day. They should just introduce themselves to your photo and video pro at the start of the wedding, so that the pros know who to ask during the event, without having to interrupt you.

- *Do you use drones?* Ask your venue first before you pay for this option, since some locations will not allow drone photography due to the noise and liabilities.
- *Who will own the copyright to our wedding photos and video?* This question is very important, since you may find that you have to order all prints through your photographer, rather than getting images on a drive and creating your own prints and enlargements. There's a big cost for prints and especially enlargements through professional photo experts, but you do get their professional-quality images that might not be achieved through some cheaper online photo processing companies.
- *How is your price determined?* By the hour, by a particular package of yours, by the number of photos shot? A flat fee will, of course, allow you to know what to expect, while a per-shot price basis could potentially floor you with the cost later.
- *What is your overtime fee?*
- *What are your travel fees?* Remember that many photo and video pros will start the clock on their time frame the minute they leave their parking lot and stop the "meter" when they get back to their offices. Ask about what constitutes their time, and when overtime will commence.
- *What will you and your assistants wear?* You'll want them to match the formality of your event, since they will be interacting with your guests.
- *What is your cancellation policy?*

As mentioned, your photo and video pros will be circulating among your wedding guests, so their personalities are something to get a feel for. A friendly, perhaps funny, photo or video pro will be best enjoyed by your guests, and of course you want to get along wonderfully with your photo and video pros, since you'll be spending a lot of time with them. I spoke with a wedding photographer recently, and she told me that she likes to spend a lot of time getting to know her couples, since she will be invited into the intimacy of their couple shots. "When the couple is comfortable with me standing right there as they're kissing, the shot comes out better." When your photographer knows you as a couple, and cares about you because of the personal connection you've struck, that comfort level and care will come through in your photos.

Ask also if your photographer will submit your wedding photos to Two Bright Lights, or other photo-gathering websites where the top bridal magazines and blogs go to find those great Real Weddings they feature. Ask what's entailed with submissions to bridal media and what you will need to do if you're willing to be submitted.

Musicians, Bands, Deejays, and Entertainers

While some couples will fly in a musician or band who is important to them, and surefire fun for their group, most other couples will hire musicians local to their destination wedding site. When interviewing any performers, keep in mind how important musical professionals are to your wedding. Your ceremony musicians set a romantic or upbeat tone for your ceremony, your reception band or deejay creates a high level of energy at your reception, and you may love the idea of having local or cultural performers adding a sense of the regional style that you love (and that helped you choose your destination wedding location in the first place!). Imagine steel pan music as your processional music, or a calypso band adding cultural flair to your reception, a mariachi band delighting guests at your welcome cocktail party, an amazing flamenco guitarist at your after-party, flamenco dancers at your reception, Irish Ceili dancers at your ceremony, Hawaiian hula dancers at your cocktail party, and more. Your location is rich with culture, no matter where your wedding is located, and it's a treat to guests to be able to enjoy a fabulous show as part of your wedding celebration.

Here are some more entertainment ideas to consider:

- Acrobats
- Aerialists
- Burlesque dancers
- Fire dancers
- Hula Hoop artists
- Ballet soloists or groups
- Opera soloists
- Harpists
- Latin dancers
- Bandura players
- Bollywood dancers
- Polynesian dancers
- Cirque du Soleil–type performers
- African dancers and drummers
- Water performers (like a mermaid or synchronized swimming group)
- And more...

Your wedding planner can help you find and interview many different kinds of entertainers who can add richness, sounds, sights, and excitement to your wedding, as well as to any wedding weekend event you'd like to plan (like having that mermaid at your welcome cocktail party poolside). You may turn up individual performers in your search, or you may find an entertainment company that employs a variety of musical performers and specialty acts.

Here are some important questions to ask of any musician, band, deejay, or specialty performer:

- *How much space do you need?* This is a crucial first question to ask, since your venue may be set up in such a way as to not allow the group or performer the required space to perform. Ask if they will perform outdoors, if that applies. Some musicians don't want their equipment exposed to the weather elements, and some dancers will require solid flooring on which to perform.
- *Do you need a stage or flooring?* You may have to rent those.
- *Do you need access to a power source?* For speakers, keyboards, and lighting equipment, many performers will need power. So be sure your venue can accommodate them, and that extension cords will be set out safely.
- *How much time will you need for setup?* If a stage will have to be constructed, you'll need to let your venue manager know when the group and their workers will need access to your wedding site. Ask also about their time needed to break down their equipment and depart. Your venue may have another wedding booked after yours, which will require your workers to be gone at a certain time or else risk a possible fee.
- *How much time will you perform?* This will take some coordinating, depending upon the length of your wedding, the venue's rules about weddings ending at a certain time (such as 10:00 p.m.), how long the band plays for each set, and how you'd like to schedule multiple acts to perform during your wedding. Get their hours in writing, including the number

and length of breaks they usually take. For bands and deejays, ask if they will play a music CD during their break(s) to keep the energy going.

- *Which instruments do your band members play?* When talented musicians play more than one instrument apiece, that provides so many more musical moments.

- *What will you wear?* The deejay or band should match the formality of your event, so if your wedding is formal, you may require that they be dressed formally as well. And since informal weddings can range in style, your entertainers will also want to be dressed appropriately, as you will want them to fit in and be photo-worthy.

- *Are your performances family-friendly?* If you'll have children present at your wedding, perhaps the burlesque dancers won't be a great idea. But you should ask your deejay or band if they can provide the edited versions of songs with explicit lyrics, if you prefer those versions for your group.

- *How many people are in your group?* In addition to the band members, you may also have to feed their crew and assistants. Deejays will often perform with assistants as well. To be sure they all get their vendor meals from your caterer, and appropriate tips from you, get a head count.

- *Can we get a copy of your playlist or a CD of your playlist?* You may want to add this to your keepsake collection of your special day.

- *Do you accept a playlist from us, including a list of songs we don't want played at our wedding?* You'll submit your song choices for special moments during your ceremony, reception, and first dances, but if you'd like

Budget Tip

A smaller number of performers will add up to fewer vendor meals, and potentially a lower fee for entertainment. That is not always the case, since some performers do charge a lot just for themselves to perform, but it can be a factor in pricing.

Planning Tip

Be sure to specify which versions of songs you'd like. Many current entertainers have covered classic songs, so let your deejay know which version you prefer, not just listing the song by name. You'll save time and money by eliminating the need for extra calls or e-mails with your deejay.

to specify any Must Play songs, be sure your performer will adhere to your list.

- *Can we see you perform during our scouting trip?* Your band, deejay, or entertainers might have an event booked during the time of your stay, one that you can safely poke your head into (not crash) to see them in action. Or, if you haven't hired them yet at the time of your early scouting trip, they may be able to audition for you.
- *Can we see video of your performances?* If you can't get to them, you'll have to rely on video they send, or videos of their work posted to their social media accounts or up on their website. Try to depend on the most recent, dated performances—which is why social media checking is important to see last weekend's wedding performance—since some video posted to websites without dates on them can be from long-ago events when the band had different members and style.
- *Will you bring in any backdrops or space-requiring items?* For nonmusical performers, such as dancers, this is an important question. Again, your layout depends on available space.
- *Will you require a room or personal space?* Some performers may need a place in which to get ready, change into costume, take breaks, do makeup, practice, and so forth.
- *Will you distribute any props during your performance?* If so, what will they be? You might not want those inflatable guitars or glow necklaces

Planning Tip

Since band members can change, with the band name remaining the same, be sure to include the names of the band members you saw at the audition in your contract. And require the band to inform you of any changes to their band personnel before your wedding day. Some bands even change styles completely, once their Motown-talented members depart. You don't want an entirely different band to show up on your wedding day, unable to play the kind of music you originally hired them for.

you've seen at other weddings, so find out what the handouts could be, or request your own types.

• *Will you invite guests to perform with you?* Some guests are happy to be pulled onto the stage to sing with the band, and you might want to surprise your partner with a song you'll sing. Some couples will take dance lessons prior to the wedding day so that they can wow their crowd by joining the professional tango dancers on the dance floor.

• *What entertainment options do we have for kids?* What can you offer for the children who will be spending time elsewhere on the premises during the adults-only wedding? Perhaps you can send a balloon artist or costumed characters to the kids' zone as a surprise and great fun for them.

• *What are your cancellation policies?*

• *If you need to cancel, will your company send another group or performer to our wedding?* Some companies will send a replacement group, if your hired singer gets strep throat or other illness, or if travel issues prevent them from reaching your location. Find a plan B performer in advance, if you're working with an entertainment company, for a possible replacement, or ask how they handle situations in which the talent cannot show up.

Beauty Experts

You'll want to look gorgeous at your wedding, as well as at your welcome cocktail party and rehearsal dinner, and your beauty team will be ready to master your chosen updo or give you that perfect makeup look for daytime. Many destination wedding brides forget about all of the additional events for which they want to look their best, and think this early in the process only about hair, makeup, and nails for the wedding itself. But I'm here to help you book your beauty pros for all of your destination wedding events now, early, before they're all booked up by other wedding groups. Your resort may have just a small beauty team, after all, and you may also find independent beauty experts at your location, or beauty salons not connected to your resort. At some destinations, there aren't many qualified beauty professionals to choose from, so early planning is key.

Here are some events for which you may want professional beauty styling:

- Your scouting trip, when you might have professional engagement photos taken of the two of you
- Your welcome cocktail party
- A night out on the town
- A day out in the sun (think amazing mermaid braids done by a pro)
- Your rehearsal dinner
- Your 2nd Look hairstyle or makeup for your reception or after-party

Your bridesmaids, moms, grandmoms, and the little girls may also want to have their hair, makeup, and nails professionally done for the wedding, likely not needing additional beauty work during the weekend or week. If you'll arrange for all of your ladies to get the royal beauty treatment, you might take over the hotel's salon, or have your beauty pros come to a suite or getting-ready area where brides and their ladies get prepped and pampered, with champagne in hand, for the big day. Many resorts will include use of a special getting-ready suite (which they know will be photographed, so it's kind of a marketing thing for them as well!), or you may need to pay for use of a getting-ready suite. You might decide to turn your own suite into the getting-ready suite, setting the stage for a gorgeous pre-party that offers some of the most enjoyable and relaxing moments before the wedding. Brides and their ladies will often have a song playlist for this getting-ready time, and the professional photographer and videographer may be present to capture this event.

So, getting back to your beauty experts, let's work on finding them for you. You'll work with your wedding planner to find the best beauty experts possible, and if you'll be at an all-inclusive or resort that offers wedding day beauty styling as part of your package, you won't have much to do. They'll offer use of their stylists, and you'll just need to find out which stylist specializes in the hair and makeup looks you want. As with any beauty group, you might find that one stylist is the "updo" specialist, while another stylist is amazing with braiding. Ask for the beauty company's recommendations when you're looking for your beauty pros.

Here are some additional questions to ask:

- *Have you done my wished-for style of hair and makeup before?* You don't want to be someone's first time with your style of updo.
- *Do you have a wedding day package that includes hair, makeup, and nails, for a discount on each?* And does your wedding package also include champagne or other treats? If not, can we bring in our own champagne and other treats?
- *Does your wedding day beauty package include a free hairstyle or other beauty service for the bride?* If I don't wish to use the freebie, can I give it to my mother? (Keep in mind that if one mom gets a freebie, any other mom should also get a freebie. So you may want to buy your future mother-in-law her updo to prevent any hurt feelings.)
- *If my bridesmaids will get their hair done in our group, is there special, discount pricing for our block of customers?* If so, does the same apply for makeup?
- *If bridesmaids arrive with their hair washed and blown out, is there a lesser charge for just doing their styling?*

- *What are the prices for "wedding hair," such as updos, that may be more expensive?* Some pros charge extra for flat-ironing and other time-consuming processes as well.
- *Can I schedule a trial run of my wedding hairstyle and makeup?* This would occur during your scouting trip or perhaps a few days prior to your wedding when you arrive early at your destination. Are trial runs free, or for a price?
- *Will my choice of hairstyle work well in the season's weather at my location?* An expert can advise you on a style that works better in the location's humidity, heat, or wind, and can potentially advise you about pre-steps to take to prevent dry hair problems. If you'd like curly hair worn loose, your stylist can create the style with setting lotion and products that can help extend the life of your look without giving you helmet hair with so much hairspray.
- *How long will my makeup last?* In hot, humid weather, and depending upon your skin's moisture levels, your makeup could be in peril of a short life span. Ask your stylists at home and on-site for any tips and products that can help your makeup look last, including setting you up with oil blotting papers and touchup products and tips.
- *Can you help me with my rehearsal dinner hairstyle and makeup look?*
- *Can you help me select a nail polish color that looks great with my wedding dress?*
- *Can you help me select a 2nd Look hairstyle for my wedding day?* Will the stylist be able to teach you how to take apart your updo and create loose, flowing curls, or should she be on hand at your wedding location to create that 2nd Look? Some couples invite their beauty stylists to the wedding itself, so they're right there for 2nd Looks and touchups.
- *How much time will you need to work on my hair and makeup on the wedding day?*
- *How much time will you need to work on each person's hair and makeup on the wedding day?*

- *How many beauty stylists will come to my location to help work on our group?*
- *Can I bring my own makeup brushes, makeup, and styling products for your use on the wedding day?* Some people prefer to use their own brushes, to avoid any possible eye infections, and they'd like to use their own makeup that their sensitive skin is used to.
- *Do you offer any additional spa treatments?* You might wish to get a massage, but avoid waxing, spray tanning, and other treatments that can cause injury or redness, an orange face, or other beauty disaster.
- *How do you handle payments and tipping?* Do you require a deposit upon booking?
- *What are your team's travel fees?*
- *What are your policies about changing our bookings or needing to cancel?*
- *Can I see your inspection certificate?* Don't be shy about asking for this, since your health is important. Anyone getting a pedicure will need to avoid infections, and you'll want to be sure the beauty center is clean and free of health violations.

Now, with your research done and your questions asked, your beauty experts hired, it's time to talk about how you'll communicate your hairstyle and makeup ideas with beauty experts who are located far away from you. For these visual effects, photos will always be the best way to communicate, especially if you have a language barrier with your on-site beauty experts. They will always want to see your choices of images that inspire you, so that they can also look at photos of you not made up, learn more about your wedding, and use images to create their plan. Create separate Hair, Makeup, and Nails Pinterest boards, and send the links to your beauty specialists so that they can see what you'd like. They might add in some images of their own, to show you what else you might consider. You can work out the details, if needed, via Skype, or save your questions for a scheduled pre-wedding trial session.

Transportation

If you'll hire a transportation company for any important rides during your wedding weekend, you'll need to find and hire a reputable transportation company that will get you there on time, in clean and good-smelling vehicles in good repair. Your resort may have a shuttle bus that will take your group to and from the airport and hotel, and your wedding group might also be granted rides to and from your rehearsal dinner in that shuttle bus so that everyone rides together. Your hotel can also help arrange limousines if that's your chosen mode of stylish transportation on the wedding day . . . and some couples book limos for the rehearsal dinner outing, needing no transportation on the wedding day.

Your hotel, whether or not you have a wedding planner booked through them, can point you to the trolley company or a yacht charter company for any other transportation you'd like for your wedding. And they can of course connect you with reputable taxis, since some regions may have unscrupulous private taxis you don't want to subject your group to, and instruct the drivers on the flat fee for your trip to any particular place.

If your wedding will take place all at one location, you won't need transportation at all, nor will you need to worry about this step or expense if your location's tradition is for a walking procession from one location to your nearby second location. These walking processions are greatly celebrated by the locals who may bestow blessings upon you, and you can't beat the looks in local children's eyes as you go walking by in your gown. You become part of the magic of the scene.

If you do wish to arrange for special transportation at any stage of your wedding getaway, here are some questions to ask:

- *Which kinds of vehicles are available for us to book?* Some companies will rent out exotic cars in addition to limos, standard limos, even Jeeps and other vehicles paired to your location.

- *Which types of vehicles are most advisable for our wedding location?* Some hilly or winding road paths are not ideal for certain types of vehicles. Smaller cars may be better than long limos, for instance.
- *Can we book a trolley just for our group, or would we have to hop on trolleys that other people use?*
- *Are your drivers experienced and licensed, and do they speak our language?*
- *Does the vehicle have a reliable GPS system, and do drivers have walkie-talkies that can be more reliable for home base communication than a cell phone?* In some regions, it can be hard to get a signal, but walkie-talkies can often do the job in a certain range.
- *What will your drivers wear?* You'll want them to be dressed close to your wedding formality level, since they will be interacting with your guests.
- *How many cars will we need?*
- *How long do we get to use the cars?* Is it a flat rate for X hours, or do you charge by the hour? Or by mileage. Get this in writing in your contract!
- *If there is a problem with the car, how long will it take to get another car sent for our use?*
- *What is your overtime policy?*
- *What is your payment schedule?* When are deposits due?
- *What is your cancellation policy?*

Planning Tip

If you'll marry at a cruise ship's port of call, you will need to arrange for transportation from the dock to the spot where your wedding will take place and back again. Make sure you arrange these rides in plenty of time to reach your wedding spot, and return to the ship in time for departure.

Think also about vehicles available for anyone in your group to drive. If you'd like to approach your beach wedding via moped or Jeep—rented for the day—you'll have to make sure your chosen drivers know the rules of the road (such as how to drive on the left-hand side of the road) and are able to rent cars or vehicles in the first place. Some locations might not rent to anyone under twenty-one, which would cause you to have to switch up your plans for a driver.

Ask if you can decorate your mode of transportation. Some companies will allow you to attach signage, such as to the back of a limo or horse and sleigh, or horse and carriage, and some will not. When a vehicle is speeding along, some signs can bounce around in the wind and chip the paint of the vehicle. So before you buy and bring car signs, make sure you have permission first. Also, ask if the vehicle will be decorated. Some horse and carriage companies festoon their carriages with flowers, and I've seen some festooned with very cheesy fake flowers, so ask about this important detail. You can ask for a non-floral carriage.

With horse-related transportation—whether carriage, sleigh, or on horseback—it's important to ask the company about their rules for the horses' safety. Some companies won't let their horses ride on highways, or in extremely hot or extremely cold weather. Find out about their rules and their cancellation policies and refunds as well, and have a Plan B in mind in case the horses can't be used for your wedding.

Watch Out!

Your mode of transportation for any wedding weekend event may be by boat. Here's an often-forgotten tip: make sure your guests bring their passports along on any sail. Some charters and boat rides will visit other nearby islands for diving, picnics, bar visits, and kayaking or hikes, and while you may start off in the Virgin Islands (where no passport is needed), you may be dropped off for a beach party on an island that isn't part of the VI. Everyone will need passports to get back. Another reason to add passport suggestions on your personal wedding website. Guests will appreciate your heads-up planning and consideration.

Rehearsal Dinner Experts

You can apply this section to any restaurant where you'll hold a wedding weekend event. You might not wish to have your rehearsal dinner at the same venue where your wedding will be, and you may have fallen in love with a romantic restaurant with a great view during your scouting trip. So ask these questions of any venue to help you select the perfect rehearsal dinner venue, or other event's setting:

- *Do you have a private party room for our event?*
- *What is the capacity of the room?* You'll want your guests to fit comfortably, not be smashed together or lost in a cavernous space.
- *If you do not have a private party room, how would you create an area in your restaurant just for our guests?* Can we have the upper floor, or a roped-off portion of your dining room?
- *How do you arrange private event menus?* Do you have a set event menu, different menus, or à la carte menu selections available?
- *Can we come in for a tasting during our scouting trip or a few days before our wedding?*
- *Does your venue also provide desserts?*
- *Can we speak with your bar manager to create a bar list and signature drinks?*
- *Do you allow décor in your venue?* How far in advance would we be able to access the party room to decorate?
- *How much time would we be allowed to use your party space?*
- *Does your restaurant have live entertainment during the time of our party?*
- *How do your deposits, payments, and tips work?*
- *Do you offer any discounts or extras for rehearsal dinner groups?*
- *Do you have any recommendations for ways to make our celebration more special?* Perhaps a special food or dessert to add to our menu?
- *Do you have a kids' menu?*

- *Do you offer specialty dishes, such as gluten-free, vegan, kosher, and other menu items?*
- *Do you do food and drink pairings?*
- *Are there any cultural dishes you can suggest for our menu?*
- *Do you charge corkage fees?* Do they apply to wine we get from you, or from outside liquor we bring to the venue for our party?
- *Do you charge cake-cutting fees?*
- *Do you have parking on-site?* If not, do you validate for parking?
- *Do you have valet service?* This might make your mobility-challenged guests happy.
- *Do you have outside seating?* Is it private for event groups?
- *Will the fire pit be lit during the season of our wedding?* (You'd be surprised how many couples book a restaurant because they love the fire pit, only to find out that the restaurant doesn't light it during certain seasons.)

Your vendor selection process is well underway. Remember to be responsive when they send you messages, getting back to them quickly and efficiently, and keep track of all agreements, orders, contracts, and communications to help your wedding plans come off smoothly, and help settle miscommunications.

10

Hotel Rooms and Details

BEFORE WE TALK about standard hotel room blocks for your guests, let me first introduce the idea of booking an estate home or villa where everyone can stay. Some resorts have, as part of their property collections, privately owned estate homes and villas that can be rented for destination weddings. And some of them are pretty fabulous! We're talking multi-million-dollar properties with private pools and private beaches, magnificent buildings with luxurious bedrooms, outdoor dining areas by the pool, tennis courts, saunas, and the owner's own butlers, personal chefs, and service staff to wait on you hand and foot. Your guests may stay with you in the estate home or villa, or you might invite a handful of VIPs to stay there while the rest of the guests stay at the resort. Whether they do or not, you will likely have access to all of the resort's amenities such as their pool, snorkeling along their shores, and free kayak rentals, as well as their dining establishments, bars, and lounges, not to mention special events like bonfires on the beach with entertainment and a gourmet buffet.

Budget Tip

Smaller villas can give you the fun of all staying together in one place, and your planner can get you that private chef experience, for less money.

Estate home and villa booking means you get the entire place to yourselves, while the resort's pools and beaches are crowded with vacationing families. Imagine treating your guests to a private dinner out at your estate's magnificent pool, overlooking a stunning sunset. That could be part of your, and your guests', wedding weekend experience. It's VIP celebrity style, a higher budget option but definitely one to look into.

While estate homes and villas may look like the perfect place to hold your wedding itself—and they are!—be sure to ask the resort or the owners themselves, since some have restrictions and insurance limitations. They may let wedding groups stay there, but weddings themselves are not allowed, by their rule. So be sure to ask first, and never try to set up your wedding in an estate home without first asking for permission, or you may be kicked out of the place, charged later for extra expenses and penalties! You and your guests might then be stranded, without places to stay. That's the epitome of a destination wedding disaster.

All right, now we can start looking at suites. Presidential suites, or whatever their top-tier rooms may be named, give you expansive space, luxurious accommodations, a bathroom to envy, a private balcony, and loads of extras like a wet bar, a fireplace, wall-length flat screen television, and other indulgences. Talk to your event planner or hotel wedding manager about booking this suite for yourselves, and do this as early in the process as possible. If the hotel has other weddings booked during the time of your stay, every other couple is going to want that room for themselves.

Now let's say the resort has multiple Presidential suites. Wouldn't it be fantastic if your parents keyed into their rooms to see that you've upgraded them to such palatial accommodations for their stay? It's a generous gift, and may be your thank-you gift to them for helping plan and pay for your wedding.

Regular room blocks should be made available to your guests, offering a nice range of room types, such as double, queen, and king-size beds, ocean views, and so on. List them on your personal wedding website with links to see the rooms. Sure, they could look on their own, but as a savvy destination wedding couple, you know that doing as much as you can to make your guests comfortable is the way to go, and providing links is an appreciated step. Set the room block up as far in advance as you can, since many guests will want to book their rooms the minute they get your Save the Date. "If we're going to have to vacation there, we want a great room" is what they're likely thinking. And they definitely want to be among those guests getting the wedding package discount room rates.

Thinking of Your Guests

Keep track of the deadline for booking rooms in your room block, and send out reminder e-mails to your guests, letting them know that if they haven't already booked their rooms, the room block booking deadline is fast approaching. You don't want the un-booked rooms to be released without guests getting fair warning, or they might blame you for not making it clear to them that a deadline loomed.

Some other pieces of information to add to your personal wedding website:

* *Check-in and check-out times.*
* *Any fees for transportation.* This includes from the airport to the resort (don't assume that there will always be a free shuttle). A necessary ferry ride to the resort may cost upward of $100 per person in some locations. Ask your resort about this, and if they say taxis are available at the airport, find out how much taxi rides are so that you can let guests know to expect a cost of around that stated amount in case fares hike before your wedding.
* *Meal plan information.* When a resort is not all-inclusive, it may have several meal plans available for guests to select from (or not select at all). Some meal plans cover all meals, some just offer breakfast and dinner, some offer breakfast and lunch, and so on. Guests need to be aware of what they will be facing as far as their meal plan choices, and also see the dining establishments and cafés at the resort to judge if they'd like to pay their own way.
* *Hotel charge rules.* Many resorts will reserve the cost of guests' stay the minute they arrive, which can take some guests by surprise when they start spending wildly at the hotel only to find out their credit cards have been maxed out. They may have planned to pay with a different card, or with several cards at the end of their stay, and this can be a very embarrassing situation when a hotel staffer shows up at their room (while friends are there) to say they have to come to the front desk to cover the cost of their stay. Don't let your guests be mortified by this common practice in resort billing. Make sure they know what to expect, and it's perfectly okay (and smart!) to add this info to your personal wedding website.
* *Availability of cribs in their rooms.*
* *Availability of handicap access rooms.*
* *Availability of non-smoking rooms.* And the hotel's rules about charges made when smoking has occurred in non-smoking rooms. This is also a

big issue if you'll stay in an estate home or private villa. Smoking might not be allowed even on their private beach.

- *Availability of adults-only beaches.* When a resort has multiple beaches due to the landscape, some resorts designate areas for families and some at which no children are allowed. Your guests might love the idea of no crying babies in the room next to theirs. Ask about the dates for this, since some resorts will drop the adults-only beach rule during off season.
- *Availability of free Wi-Fi.* Some resorts don't have it, especially in some more remote destination wedding locations. Guests need to know if there will be a free access code for them to use, and guests with kids will really need to know this for their kids' tablet use during their stay.
- *Parking fees.* Some resorts don't charge their guests for parking, and some do. Make sure guests know which one it is so they can plan their budget accordingly.
- *Resort freebies.* Let them know about the free kayak rentals at the resort that they might use for their downtime, as well as any other freebies the resort or your wedding package offers. For the guests' use, I mean. Not that you're getting a free wedding cake!
- *Availability of rooms located away from the ballroom or pool area.* Some resorts have "quiet" areas for guests' comfort, which some of your guests will greatly appreciate.
- *Spa menus.* Guests may want to treat themselves, and advance booking—especially during peak season—can get them in the door.
- *Dress code information for restaurants at which you'll have events.* Some fine restaurants require men to wear jackets and ties, or button-down shirts, for instance. Make sure your guests know what to pack so that they don't feel uncomfortable at your event. I've seen more restaurants with "no sneakers" and "no flip-flops" rules, and I've seen people turned away at the door for wearing sneakers. Some places are tough.
- *Anything else you'd like to include.* Review your itinerary for the entire wedding weekend so that guests may know that you plan a group

Thinking About Your Guests

Consider adding even a small denomination gift card to your resort in each guest welcome goodie bag. Guests can use it any way they wish, from antacids at the gift shop to "lunch on you" at the café to part of their spa treatment.

snorkeling outing via catamaran. When they know what you have planned, they won't be likely to book a snorkeling outing for themselves the day before yours.

Check with your wedding planner about what he or she might be able to arrange for your hotel stay. Some planners known to the hotel have a certain amount of pull, through their great relationship with the hotel or resort, and that can create terrific opportunities like room upgrades, a discount on the welcome cocktail party, and more . . . all because your planner is on your team. I've heard that some planners have such a great amount of pull that they can make one phone call and get a hotel room block arranged when the resort said to the calling-direct couple that they had no rooms available. No, they're not getting another wedding bumped. Some hotels just hold a bunch of rooms open for special circumstances. Your wedding could be that special circumstance.

Again, book your hotel rooms early, because there may be conventions in town, a large wedding also staying at the hotel, family reunions, and other groups snapping up all of the best rooms.

Now what if you're not having your wedding at the hotel at which you'd like to stay? You'd love for that resort to be your wedding group's "home," but your wedding will take place at a nearby restaurant with a view of the luxury yacht–lined marina. Call, or have your planner call, to say that you'd like X number of rooms for a wedding group, and the sales manager may be just as likely to grant your booking. Do this early on, and make sure those bookings are guaranteed.

Hotel Room Goodie Bags

They're pretty much a Must at destination weddings. Guests keying into their rooms will look for them and perhaps be puzzled if they don't find one. Some guests even get offended, thinking everyone else got one but them. People are funny like that.

For your destination wedding goodie bag, think about—you guessed it—your guests' experience and comfort level first. If yours is a location that naturally has a lot of mosquitoes, include mosquito sprays and wipes for guests' use. Sunblock sticks are also a great idea in any locale, even in snowy ones. You've got to block those UV rays everywhere! And my third pick for comfort item is fluffy socks or spa socks for guests to slip on, keeping feet warmer on cold winter mornings and also to provide comfort for those guests who have a "thing" about walking barefoot on hotel room carpeting and tile flooring. Even in the best five-star hotels, guests may bring with them a long-standing fear of hotel room floors. So socks are the answer.

Add in that gift card you read about just a moment ago, and include a note from you encouraging guests to use this card on your hotel's allowable amenities. Find out first if there are any restrictions, such as no gift cards allowed for spa treatments. It's rare to see that particular No, but you wouldn't want a guest to get an unwelcome surprise at paying time.

Bottles of water are always a prized destination wedding goodie bag item, especially if your wedding will be held in a region where water safety is questionable.

Don't Forget

Don't forget to include sunblock, snacks, and pairs of socks for any kids traveling with your guests, even if they won't be at your wedding.

Be generous and give multiple bottles for your guests' use. Bottled and canned soda is also a treat, and freebie mixes for any liquors they'll pull from the mini bar. Little bottles of liquor are also on the radar for prized goodie bag finds.

Additional items to include in your goodie bags:

- *Printed itinerary.* Add a printout for your wedding weekend events, with a dress code reminder.
- *Note.* A hand-written note from you, welcoming guests to your wedding weekend.
- *Packaged snacks.* You get extra Awesome Wedding Couple points if you arrange for your gluten-free guests to get gluten-free snacks.
- *Breath mints.* We all need them when we're drinking and eating spicy or garlicy foods.
- *Dental floss.* It's something guests will often forget to pack, and an appreciated item.
- *Stomachache remedies.* Antacids, or gingered candy can offer possible relief.
- *Something for the little ones.* Toys and games for kids.
- *Laminated dive card.* This is one of my favorite finds in destination wedding goodie bags for island weddings where snorkeling and glass-bottom kayaking is on the itinerary. A laminated card IDs the fish and sea life your guests might see while underwater. The card comes with them, or stays in a beach bag, to give them the excitement of IDing their spotted sea crea-

tures. They may also now know what a barracuda looks like, in order to avoid one.

- *A fresh flower.* Tied to the bag, welcoming guests with a sensory experience from the location.

You might also want to consider arranging for guests to find platters of fresh fruit, crackers, tapenade, hummus, and other edibles in their rooms, together with a bottle of wine, pitcher of sangria, or other coordinated drink pairing. They can kick back and have a little party during their first moments there. You'd make a stellar first impression on your destination wedding weekend. Travel can make people hungry and cranky, so your foodie gift can boost their mood as well.

11

Planning Your Wedding Weekend Events

REV UP YOUR guests' excitement even more with well-planned wedding weekend events. Your guests, after all, have come a long way to attend your wedding. This trip may be their one annual vacation. They've stepped away from their demanding work and personal schedules in tribute to your relationship. So spoil them a bit with all of your additional events (besides your wedding).

Your Arrival Cocktail Party

When guests arrive, they'll get their first treat in the form of the goodie bags you've had placed in their hotel rooms, or that welcoming platter of cheese, fruit, and crackers if you've opted for a bit of a spread instead. That's a little something just for them. Soon after, they'll make their way to the welcome cocktail party you've planned just for them, likely the first

Beaches have an undeniable romantic attraction. Cape May, New Jersey, provides the perfect backdrop for Leah and Chris's sunny, breezy celebration.
Photos by Two 17 Photo & Cinema

A colorful taxi is
a must-get photo at
a city destination wedding.

The pop of color in those
gorgeous shoes against
the gray cityscape
makes for a vibrant shot.
Photos by Two 17 Photo & Cinema

Beaches can inspire a wide range of wedding decorations. *Photo by Danielle Richards Photography*

This sun-drenched pier seems to cry out for a photo-op. *Photo by Joseph Toris*

Sparkling lights from a beach wedding reception on St. John, USVI.

Rainbows are a comm sight at island weddir one that many weddi couples wish for.
Photos by Kati Bradl of Sail Kalina

Latitude and longitude make for a clever wedding memento.

38° 71' 98" N   79° 09' 53" W

paradise

A globe can also represent the location of a destination wedding.
Photos by Two 17 Photo & Cinema

Street names can give local flavor
to your table location markers.

Here, the table number
reflects a nautical theme.
Photos by Two 17 Photo & Cinema

neel Bay on St. John, USVI,
has been the scene of many
a lovely wedding reception.
Photos by Joseph Toris

The Statue of Liberty raised her torch
as if saluting Rebecca and Ryan
at their NYC destination wedding.

A luxury yacht gave the bride and groom
plenty of space for their celebration and
a quiet place for a moment alone.
Photos by Danielle Richards Photography

oard the *Aqua Azul*—part of the
ooth Sailing Celebrations fleet of
ury yachts—often chartered for weddings.

A sweet and romantic moment
for Rebecca and Ryan.
Photos by Danielle Richards Photography

Fun and easy-to-bring-along
Bride and Groom props
let you add your personalitie
to your day, then take them
home to use happily ever afte

Thoughtful items for guests' use
help make a destination wedding
a hit. This basket of hankies
is ready for the tears of joy
they'll shed during your day.
Photos by Two 17 Photo & Cinema

A stunningly colorful
fall wedding scene
in Connecticut.

This timeworn bridge
in its peaceful forest setting
seems perfect for wedding photos
or as a ceremony location.
Photos by Joseph Toris

Quiet moments on the beach at sunset create perfect photo opportuni
Remember to build downtime into your destination wedding sched
Photo by Sharon Na

The little details in a stunning
destination wedding setting
bring local charm to your big day.
This statue in a New Orleans
garden watches over the celebration.
Photo by Sharon Naylor

A beautifully lit courtyard
brings character and charm
to the cocktail party.
*Photo by Two 17 Photo
& Cinema*

This shot of the wedding couple
lounging in front of a stunning
blue ocean hours before their ceremony
conveys the relaxing nature of
an island destination wedding.

A colorful koi pond adds bea
—and the sound of a waterfal
to an exotic destination wedding setti
Photos by Sharon Nay

Freshly picked island flowers
shared their natural beauty
and sweet scent during the
wedding ceremony.
Photo by Joseph Toris

Plan a morning sail for your destination wedding
group, on a day other than your wedding day,
for an unforgettable and photo-worthy outing.
Photo by Sharon Naylor

Sugar mill ruins, found on many destination wedding islands, can be the settings for your rehearsal dinner, cocktail party, welcome party, or wedding

A dazzling island sunset may provide nature's finest light show for your island wedding. *Photos by Joseph Toris*

time all of your guests will be together and such a moment of elation for you when each guest arrives. It's also a moment of bonding for your guests who will become fast friends if they aren't already—and maybe sparks will fly between singles!

Maybe you were able to greet each ferry or shuttle upon guests' arrival for a first hug and handshakes, or perhaps not. But this is the official kickoff of your wedding weekend, a celebration that sets a high bar for the rest of the weekend to surely surpass.

Here are a few details to consider:

* *Remember, all destination wedding guests should be invited to your welcome cocktail party.* This is not a rehearsal dinner to which you might invite just the bridal party. Destination weddings are all about inclusion, without any perceived favoritism. So everyone gets invited, even the kids who will not be in attendance at your actual wedding.
* *Work with your resort's event planner/your wedding planner to make your party official.* Make sure the planner reserves private areas or rooms, terraces, rooftop bars, or poolside for your party. Other groups at your resort will do so, even if you got there first with your tiki torches and set that area up for your event. The resort will kick you out and let the group who planned officially take that space. So always plan your wedding weekend events with the resort's wedding planner or event team involved fully for the best sites to be reserved for you, and their best servers assigned to your party.

Budget Tip

Some resorts, with the help of your wedding planner, will thank you for booking your wedding by throwing in an extra few dishes, or desserts, or discount pricing, for your welcome cocktail party.

- *Plan those cocktails.* The cocktail party is not something to throw together, such as by just having everyone meet at the bar. It will be better to plan your event in a space reserved for you, with an official menu and drinks list, smartly planned with the help of your event planning team, the chefs and bar manager, and even the resort's floral team for sweet décor at your party.
- *Choose a great location.* Have you planner reserve the perfect spot for your cocktail party, such as the outdoor terrace of a restaurant, a private party room in a stately manor, a rooftop bar, a section of beach reserved for your party, the pool area of your resort (marked Private Event for your guests only), a yacht.
- *Plan a menu of light bites.* Feature location-inspired food mixed with cocktail party classics, so that all of your guests' preferences are met.
- *Decide how extravagant you'd like to be.* It's perfectly fine to offer a half dozen passed hors d'oeuvres types, plus a few buffet menu items, and limit your bar offerings to just wine and beer for this opening act. After a day of travel, guests may enjoy the ease of snacking while mingling, and they understand that a limited bar list now is simply the warm-up to greater drinks to come.
- *Arrange for live entertainment.* Ask the manager if the hotel already has live entertainment booked for their bar. They may offer steel drum music as a regular feature, and your party held in the same venue means you get

Destination Wedding Etiquette

Take a moment to welcome all of your guests, thanking them for taking time out of their busy lives and traveling all this way to be with you. This expression of gratitude goes a long way with guests who have had long travel days and have perhaps sacrificed attending other events to make it to your wedding. With those kind words spoken and guests honored, the fun may begin.

free entertainment. If not, talk with your wedding planner about bringing in a musical artist to play your party. The hotel's wedding planner likely has a list of their favorite performers, and you can "audition" them online through videos on their websites before hiring.

Alternative Welcome Cocktail Parties

If you'd like to go beyond the traditional cocktail party setup held at the hotel, you might opt to plan this event at another location. Some ideas to consider:

* *A nearby restaurant.* Choose a location with an amazing view different from the one at your hotel. It may be a restaurant located high above an island vista with views of other islands, a marina filled with luxury yachts, or a garden setting.
* *An al fresco gathering in the location's setting.* Perhaps tables set up in a nearby vineyard. This option may let you use your second choice of wedding style. Let's say you chose a hotel ballroom for your wedding, but you really loved the idea of a vineyard wedding. When the logistics don't work out for the vineyard as your wedding celebration (perhaps it's booked for the next day, for instance), you can now have that dreamy vineyard setting celebration as part of your getaway wedding dream! Keep this option in mind for your second choice style—vineyard or not. It's a terrific way to get both of your top choices in the mix.
* *Host your welcome party at a nearby brewery.* Try something a little different. Guests can tour the brewery and enjoy custom-chosen brews along with food pairings.
* *Host your welcome party at a nearby museum.* Many museums welcome private parties after-hours. Your guests will be treated to gorgeous works of art, some history of your location, and the wedding-elevating style of an unexpected venue.

• *Host your welcome party aboard a yacht.* Again, if you decided against the yacht wedding, this unforgettable onboard party with stunning views, delectable food, and flowing drinks can be a location-perfect, style-choice-satisfying, and photo-worthy option.

Wedding Morning Breakfast/Brunch

No, not the morning-after breakfast. Not yet. This wedding weekend event is for the morning of the wedding. And it might be two or three separate events. Here's what I mean: it would be wonderful to plan a special breakfast or brunch for all of your wedding guests to enjoy in a great setting, such as a party room or a roped-off section of the hotel's restaurant. They get to choose from a lavish brunch buffet, or choose their favorite dishes from a custom menu you've arranged with the hotel.

You both can certainly attend this brunch with your guests, if you wish. But if you wish to follow tradition and not see each other before the ceremony, you can arrange for breakfast or brunch to be served to each of you and your attendants where you will be getting ready. So imagine a brunch spread in a fabulous suite that serves as your "home base" for the wedding morning, with plenty of champagne or mimosas on pretty platters. Plus a tray of petits fours or other dessert for some morning sweets. Your partner's group also gets their own spread, perhaps with a different customized menu and list of drinks.

This morning breakfast provides quality time for your inner circle, and makes sure that everyone has eaten something for stamina and for the ability to enjoy some bubbly or cocktails without getting tipsy. This is a prime photo-taking event, so think about having your professional photographer show up early for this morning-sun event. Play some music from your specially chosen playlist, and enjoy those moments before your ceremony is set to begin.

After-Party

Continue the celebration after your reception comes to an end with your after-party. Some resorts have a rule about weddings ending at 10:00 p.m., and your group will certainly want to continue on. Think also about afternoon wedding timing. If your reception ends at 5:00 p.m., the party can continue elsewhere for many hours afterward.

Just like with your wedding day breakfast, you can plan one event for everyone to attend, or plan separate events. For instance, you and your friends may wish to hop on a shuttle and head into a nearby town for some club-hopping or take over the hotel bar, while your parents and their friends grab some drinks out on the hotel's terrace or back in their suite. It's completely up to you (and them). The older generations might not relish the idea of late-night bar-hopping, but instead may want to stay at the hotel for relaxed time with their loved ones. Everyone gets to do what they wish for the perfect close to your wedding day.

Here are some after-party ideas to consider:

- A cocktail party by the hotel's pool, reserved for your group
- A cocktail party on a rooftop
- An outing to a local restaurant for champagne and desserts or late-night bites

- A sunset sail post-afternoon wedding, with live music, food, and drinks on board
- A bonfire on the beach, with permission and permits, of course
- Hot tubbing at the ski lodge, or a swim in your suite's private pool
- Star-gazing in a national park, with catered food and drinks or upscale picnic baskets
- Going to see live music in the hotel's lounge or at a nearby restaurant
- Going dancing at a well-known club or at your hotel's after-hours club
- After-dinner drinks tasting with food pairings

Here's a question you may be asked about your afternoon wedding's after-party. This is the one that starts at 5:00 p.m. after your noon wedding. Guests who brought their kids along to your location but had a sitter watch the kids during the wedding may ask if they can bring their kids to the after-party. It sounds like a ridiculous idea—who would bring a four-year-old club-hopping?! But if the after-party has been listed on your personal wedding website as a bonfire on the beach with s'mores and games, those parents may see no issue with having the kids attend. It's up to you if you'll allow kids to jump into your post-wedding party, or if you'd like to keep it adults-only. Guests may have been drinking since the morning, so what would those kids observe of your more inebriated guests? You know

Budget Tip

Talk to your hotel's manager or wedding planner about your wish to have your after-party at the hotel. When you decide this early, perhaps at the time of booking, you may be offered other perks or discounts, beside a budget-friendly group rate for your additional event. And some hotels may even agree to bring out extra slices of your wedding cake at this second party, getting double the use from it and creating a budget freebie for your champagne and dessert party. The champagne may be from your reception's bar collection as well, bottles you've already paid for. Cheers to that!

your crowd, and may predict milder behavior, but what about those +1s you don't know? It may be better to plan a late-day or nighttime event for the kids—perhaps a movie/pizza night and pajama party in a hotel room, organized by the hotel or your wedding planner, with sitters ready to watch the kids until the wee hours. You may even have a second shift of sitters for this post-party for the kids. It's definitely an idea to consider.

Morning-After Breakfast

And here we are at the morning-after breakfast, one last chance to treat your guests to a wonderful meal before they head back home. As you know, the catered morning-after breakfast has been a frequent and expected event for many years, but for destination weddings, it may be a bit different. This type of wedding will often have many of your guests waking up very early to take a red-eye home, or departing at sunrise to drive before heavy traffic delays their trip back home. Guests loved your getaway wedding and hate to miss out on what will surely be a fabulous morning-after breakfast. But they've gotta catch their plane or hit the road.

And then there are your guests who drank way too much the night before and couldn't stomach breakfast the next day. They would surely be no-shows at your catered breakfast.

So here are your three possibilities to keep yourself safe from over-spending on guests whose travel schedules and alcohol tolerance you couldn't know ahead of time:

1. *Plan an official breakfast event.* Provide for guest access to the hotel's breakfast buffet or your own custom menu, but arrange ahead of time with your hotel for per-person charges according to who shows up. No firm RSVPs needed.
2. *Just let guests know when breakfast is served.* Or they can go when they wish. Some might show up at 7:00 a.m. when breakfast is served, and

some might show up to brunch at 10:00 a.m. They get the freedom to make their own schedules, which they may appreciate because they won't have to wake up early to get to your planned breakfast when their flight out isn't until noon.

3. *Arrange for in-room delivery.* Have breakfast treat–filled picnic baskets, coffee, and juice delivered to their rooms that morning, so that they can dine privately on their terraces or in their rooms. It's a breakfast surprise.

I remember a wedding trip we took to Antigua, which allowed us to just go to breakfast whenever we liked. We said we were with the wedding group, and we were handed special menus. An extra delight was a "signature drink" of freshly made blueberry juice, which was hands down the best juice I'd ever had in my life. That last burst of special indulgence painted the entire wedding event more amazing in my eyes, since the couple and their hotel went to such great effort to line up such wonderful little details at this final stop in the wedding adventure.

Breakfast may be included in the all-inclusive, which makes this a terrific option for parents to host, since it won't drain them financially, and you also have the option to host this morning-after breakfast without worry about the bill. Champagne, mimosas, Bloody Marys, and other alcoholic drinks might not be on the all-inclusive menu, so ask ahead of time about how the hotel would bill for that.

Think About Your Guests

Keep this event local, at the hotel. Given guests' needs to travel that morning, they'd prefer to stick close to their rooms. Going to a separate location's restaurant, no matter how gorgeous, can complicate things for your guests and may prevent them from being able to attend.

Keep it casual, and allow guests a nice window to make their own schedules for breakfast (say, between 8:00 a.m. and 1:00 p.m.), and be sure to visit guests at each table during this last event. Favors may be handed out—perhaps a treat for the road and a bottle of water with your personalized labels (leftovers from your reception are fine to give out now!).

You'll have your breakfast options listed on your personal wedding website and on the printed itinerary you've enclosed in your guests' welcome baskets. And here's a note to add: be sure to include a suggestion for guests to double-check and confirm their flight information the day before departure, since some airlines (particularly overseas) have been known to change or cancel flights. Maybe some guests receive text alerts on their phones about flight changes, but some might not have that app capability. So you would save the day when your note helps guests find out flight changes or cancellations with plenty of time to make other plans.

Additional Wedding Weekend Events

Fill your wedding weekend with extra activities, to enable your guests to get that vacation experience they crave, and also to give you an excellent amount of Fun Time with your friends and family. Before we get into listing out some ideas for your outside-the-wedding time, bear in mind that when you invite guests to an activity that has a price tag attached (like the resort's sunset champagne sail at $55 per person, or swimming with turtles at $40 per person), it's best for you to cover those costs when it's a planned event for the entire group. You don't want guests showing up on the dock for the sunset cruise, only to find out it's going to cost them over $100 per couple.

Now it is possible to get that swimming with turtles experience with your friends if you first inform them of the price. Here is the wording to use on your personal wedding website's itinerary: "On Friday afternoon, anyone who'd like to join us on our outing to the Swim with Turtles center is more than welcome! Please see their website for pricing and rules." They'll probably get the picture

Real Life Story

"While many of the other guests signed on for a winery tour, some of my cousins and I decided to go out into the village to do some ancestry searching, since we were in Italy and had never been able to get here for our own ancestry research. We had a terrific morning, visiting the church where our great-grandparents got married, and happened upon a little bistro with the best lunch! It was a terrific choice!"

—Carina, wedding guest

from that, but in case you'd like to be super-careful, add: "The price is $40 per person, $20 per child, and you can send your check ahead of time to me to reserve your spot."

A guest may choose not to attend a for-pay event, and that's okay! A great wedding weekend provides many pockets of downtime for guests who would rather lie on the beach, soaking up the sun, or take a little trip into town to do some shopping with other guests. That makes it more of a vacation for them, and avoids the sense of "obligatory fun" that many guests might not enjoy. So let guests relax and make their own decisions.

Some additional outings to consider:

- Catamaran rides to go snorkeling at a choice beach, with drinks served on board or at a stop at a beach bar
- Jeep tours of the island
- Visits to wineries
- Biking tours
- Shopping outings
- Touristy bus tours to take in all the celebrity homes and Hollywood hotspots
- Spa time for your group

- Skiing and snowboarding, with the non-sporting types enjoying the ski lodge bar and restaurant
- Festivals going on at the time of your wedding
- Theater and concert outings
- Attending a sporting event in a nearby stadium
- Casino visit
- Yoga on the beach at sunrise or sunset
- Tennis tournament for your group
- Golf outing
- Surfing lessons
- Basketball game
- Croquet or cricket, trying out the local sport
- Professionally shot photo sessions of families and individuals at your location or at a scenic spot, or a planned Selfie Outing at which guests can shoot their own photos in a gorgeous location. Some professional photographers can take photos underwater, which would allow for lots of creativity in guest photos. Add in costumes (such as a mermaid tail) and it's the underwater equivalent of a photo booth, which guests will love for their social media posts.
- Nature walks with a guide pointing out fascinating plants, trees, flowers, stone formations, and animals/birds/butterfly types.

These are just some of the outings you can plan during your destination wedding weekend, and do feel free to plan several. Guests, of course, can decide which they'd like to attend. Be sure to mix up the times of your planned events, since some guests may be early birds primed for a pre-breakfast hike and some may not wake until noon but would certainly love late-night pub crawling.

Not every wedding weekend activity has to be a group activity. Talk to your hotel manager or wedding planner about the possibility of arranging special discounts to the hotel spa for your wedding group. A percentage off can make the fees doable for your guests, another nice treat from you. If the hotel can't grant a

Destination Wedding Etiquette

Include your wedding weekend events to which all guests will be invited on your personal wedding website so that guests know about them and can arrange their plans accordingly, such as making plans for a side trip with their friends. Some events they may plan could include ordering tickets to attractions or events, so you wouldn't want them to find out later that you booked that time for them. If others will host events for all guests, be sure to include their contact information for RSVPs on your personal wedding website, but if their events will be just for their friends only, keep it off your website and allow them to send out their own invitations. Get your personal wedding website up as soon as possible to achieve the best wedding etiquette possible: keeping guests in the know.

spa discount—often, spas are independent entities from the hotel—ask about the possibility of arranging a spa goodie bag for your guests who do book treatments there. The spa might already offer them, making it free for you.

And again, sometimes the best thing you can do for your guests is to leave them alone. Let them have romantic downtime, friends and family downtime, some breathing room that they want for this getaway that's also their vacation. A hectic lineup of activities is not everyone's style, and keep in mind that you'll need lots of downtime during the wedding weekend, too. So set up a few events, but be sure to leave a fair amount of time open each day.

12

Planning Your Ceremony

IT'S TIME TO work on the heart of your destination wedding: your wedding ceremony. Even when your marriage license is already signed and official, as may be the legalities for the location of your wedding, your ceremony brings the beauty and the meaning to your wedding. It's when you incorporate traditions and your faith connection, speak heartfelt words of promise and appreciation to one another, and exchange those perfect rings and seal your vows with a kiss. It's the magic at the core of your marriage, made all the more magical by the location in which you marry. You may have chosen to have a destination wedding just for this dream, taking your vows in a breathtaking setting, in the feel of an exotic culture or a connection to your ancestors. For so many reasons, planning your ceremony has to be a very high priority for your destination wedding. It is, after all, the centerpiece of your entire wedding, and the center of your marriage.

I can't emphasize enough how important it is to get current and accurate information on the legalities of marrying via a destination wedding. Look to chapter 15 ("Legalities") for guidelines on where to check, who

129

to ask, and what you might choose to do to skip the whole red tape mess of getting married overseas. Since other countries and islands will often have their own rules about permissions, licenses, waiting periods, fees, and even some archaic rules about medical tests, you'll need to be sure you go through all official channels and fulfill all requirements to make sure your marriage is legal, not just where you married but when you come back home. That said, let's start planning your dreamy wedding ceremony.

Choosing Your Ceremony Style

Will you have a religious ceremony, complete with all of the religious elements that mean so much to the two of you, and in keeping with the rules of a house of worship at your destination? Will you have an interfaith wedding, again with all of the religious elements that mean so much to the two of you, and in keeping with the coordinated rules of a house of worship and with the rules of your officiants? Or will you have a civil ceremony, with no religious elements and formed in part by the rules of the civil office and the practices of your civil officiant?

The decision rests in your connections to your faiths, and how important it is to have your marriage recognized by your faith or house of worship. You will need to search your souls to figure out if your religion will play a role in your ceremony, and in assessing that, you might receive input from your parents with their strong or subtle opinions on how you should marry. This can often be a stumbling block for many couples who wish to conform to the traditions of their families but who might not feel a genuine connection to their faith. So take some time now to talk about how big a role your faiths will play in your ceremony.

When marrying couples start exploring religious, interfaith, and spiritual ceremonies, they often find that there is a world of variety when it comes to their destinations' religious and spiritual rules, those rites that you might find are non-negotiable with some religious and interfaith officiants. You might be aware that here at home, some houses of worship will not send one of their religious officiants to conduct an outdoor wedding, since they require that all of their sanctioned marriages be blessed inside a house of worship. When you start looking into the religious rules of other cultures, you might start seeing lists of rules that can be unrealistic to fit into your wedding timetable. It can all get very overwhelming.

So to help you decide, if you're wavering, here are some details to consider about each type of wedding style:

Religious

- A religious wedding ceremony is conducted by a religious officiant and includes various religious rites to unite you.
- There may be differences between the prayers you know from your home church and the prayers, wording, and rites in a church of the same religion but in another culture or country, something to keep in mind.
- You will probably want to ask for scripts from their religious ceremonies to get a feel for the formality, level of religion, wording, and rituals you may be required or encouraged to include.

- Some religious officiants hold tight to the values and rites of their church, but will be willing to discuss your wishes and work with you to customize your ceremony. In some cases, they may need to seek permission from a higher level of their church, which can take some unexpected time.
- You may run into restrictions on which types of music can be played at your ceremony, which readings, and so on. It's important to ask any religious leader or house of worship manager for any lists of restrictions and any clarification on what can and can't be included in a ceremony before you book the church and pay a non-refundable deposit.
- For interfaith weddings, you may face double the legwork when you have to interview two separate religious officiants, or your wedding planner may be able to direct you to interfaith wedding "teams" who have conducted many weddings together. These types of connections by your wedding planner can be very valuable, and can help you avoid a mess of rules in the first place. You may be better able to customize your ceremony with a coordinated meeting with the two officiants, perhaps via Skype or during a sit-down meeting on your pre-visit or a few days prior to your wedding.
- In some countries, interfaith marriages aren't considered binding or legitimate, so research this well with the help of your wedding planner. Some couples who face this seeming brick wall opt to marry officially before their getaway wedding, with their marriage recognized by their church, and then have a ceremony conducted by an interfaith or independent officiant at their destination wedding without worrying about rules or legitimacy. They just love the style of their chosen interfaith officiants and have them lead the ceremony through its beautiful elements.
- You are encouraged to find out what the rules of your overseas house of worship are about your individual faiths and their permission to marry. In some countries, although it may seem unthinkable to you, some houses of worship will not grant ceremonies to interfaith couples. You may be asked to convert before they'll allow you to marry within their walls.

Spiritual Ceremony

- There's no preference for the inclusion of religious rites or religious permissions at this type of wedding. Your spiritual officiant will help you design your ceremony to include your own spiritual beliefs, which may include elements of nature or your own understanding of a greater power.
- While friends and family may be included in any style of wedding, from religious to civil, this type of wedding opens the doors to friends and relatives reading spiritual poems and prayers, and without strict religious rules about music that can be played at a ceremony, this type of wedding may invite special musical performances by your own loved ones.
- You might ask to see scripts of wedding ceremonies conducted by any spiritual or independent officiant, so that you know how spiritual they get. Some officiants may be a little bit "out there," which can lead to chuckles from your guests when you're all unexpectedly faced with summoning of spirits, sprites, and other mystical beings as a part of your ceremony. Get a feel for their content, and meet with your officiant ahead of time to help direct your ceremony elements.

Civil Ceremony

- A civil ceremony contains no religious elements, and conforms to the scripts and rules of the justice of the peace office or other legal establishment where you will find those who are legally able to conduct wedding ceremonies and make them official.
- When you meet with the marriage registrar or official who will conduct your ceremony, you may be given a packet of information on the office's wedding scripts and requirements. Always ask for this information, and remember that when it comes to getting any official rules about your wedding from websites, that information might not be current. Even if a civil wedding office's rules are posted online, rules can change before their administrator

can make the change to their website. Ask a manager at the office for the current rules and information, and—important!—ask if there are any changes coming up that you need to know or need to check back on.

Pre-Ceremony Details

Think about making a lovely first impression for your guests. Yes, they'll surely be impressed with the gorgeous setting and décor for the ceremony, but when they are greeted by servers with silver trays bearing champagne and berries, or a signature drink chosen just for your ceremony, it's a VIP-style welcome. Circulating personal servers is one style of drink sharing, and you can also set up a drink bar or station, such as with spiked cider or hot chocolate for a fall or winter wedding, or flavored iced teas for a spring or summer setting.

Guests may also be welcomed by personalized signs, which you'll have placed in spots leading them to your ceremony location and once they arrive. You've seen those "pick a seat, not a side" signs on Instagram and Pinterest, and you may wish to create or order signs with more originality and more of your personalities. A heartfelt welcome or something with a touch of your humor send a message of happiness that your guests have joined you.

Music

Depending on your chosen ceremony site—such as a church with rules about which types of music may be played—you'll select musical performers and songs for your processional, during the ceremony, and for your recessional, and don't forget about songs you'd like played while guests are arriving.

It's a great touch for a destination wedding to choose traditional songs from your destination's culture to set the tone for your ceremony in its location, a way to pay homage to your love for this setting and to tailor your ceremony to the tone of your surroundings. For instance, if your ceremony will take place in an Italian village, consider some Italian operatic music. If you'll be in a castle, consider royal wedding–style trumpet or organ music, a grand statement that sets the mood. In Mexico, consider mariachi music, and on a Caribbean island, steel pan music is ideal. Now since a destination wedding is not always in a foreign country or on an island—perhaps your wedding away is in California wine country or at a mountain resort an hour from your home—you're free to choose any style of music you'd like, from classic ceremony songs to contemporary music, single musician music like guitar or a trio of string instruments. The music in your ceremony says a lot about who you are as a couple, and simply enhances the beauty of this big moment to come.

Here are some tips to arranging for your destination wedding ceremony's music:

• *Talk to your wedding planner or your venue's manager*. Ask them about the types of musicians who often play at weddings at their location. The venue may have an approved list of musicians who may be hired. An expert familiar with the setting can also tell you which types of instruments "play well" in that setting, such as informing you that string instruments or flute get drowned out by the sound of ocean surf.

- *Audition performers during your pre-wedding visit.* You may luck out and spot a wedding taking place on the bluff during your stay. If you love the sound of that wedding's musical performers, the venue's manager can get you their contact information, or the information for that wedding's co-ordinator. If there isn't a wedding taking place, ask for a list of recommended musicians, or look on the site's blog for their Real Wedding stories in which musicians are credited. Set up times for auditions. The hotel may allow you to use an empty meeting room for your "tryouts."

- *Can you simply look at videos of the group online?* Keep in mind that bands often "change faces" as some performers leave the band and new ones arrive. So that video you're seeing may be what the band looked and sounded like a few years ago. So even though it sounds like an efficient move, the intel you get might be outdated. You may have better luck looking on the musicians' social media pages for video of their performances last weekend, but again, a fresh look is always best, if possible.

- *Ask about and check for your musicians' access to a power source.* If your wedding will take place out in a field, how would performers who need electricity power up? A wedding planner will often look for these fine details, so it's always a good idea to have your planner there with you for venue scouting. (Caterers and other pros may need power, too, so be sure you're aware of what it will take to get them the power sources they need, and enough of them, with enough amps to fulfill their tasks. Some older venues may not be able to provide enough wattage and will thus need a generator.)

- *Ask about noise restrictions at your venue.* Many resorts and sites have noise curfews, such as weddings ending at 10:00 p.m. to provide quiet for other hotel guests, for instance. Will your plan for electronic dance music to the wee hours be shut down early? Speaking of noise, could there be another wedding nearby whose music can be heard from yours? If the site you're looking at has a public beach right around the bend of the shoreline, and that public beach often is home to loud parties, their blasting music could be heard from your location. Ask the site's event team for details on nearby noise possibilities.

- *Add to your plan B ideas a way to provide shelter for your musicians.* Entertainers don't want their pricy instruments and speakers doused in a rainstorm. A musician's tent is a good idea to have on standby.
- *Find out if musicians need a sturdy surface on which to perform.* Keyboardists, steel pan players, cellists, and other musicians may require a stage or surface on which to play. You may have to rent one.
- *Ask about the availability of a sound system.* A hotel may likely have a sound system of their own that you can use, but in a non-hotel location like a villa or a beach you may have to rent mics and speakers so that guests can hear not just the music but your vows. Again, those crashing waves can drown out all sound even at a surprising proximity.
- *List your ceremony songs in your program.* Guests always want to know what that delightful song was, and if you have a personal story about why you chose that song—perhaps it's a traditional wedding song in your location's culture, or it was played at your grandparents' wedding—share that as well for an extra-special touch to your ceremony.

Readings

You will, of course, work with your officiant about appropriate and suggested readings to include in your ceremony, and you'll likely spend time online looking up terrific ceremony readings and poetry. You may have a poem that's special to the two of you, and you can also be the author of a poem that is to be read at your ceremony. Quite often at destination weddings, the readings are inspired at least in part by the location. It might be a poem by that country's poet laureate or a native artist, or it might be a reading that talks about the beauty of nature, tying in your lovely setting.

Outside of traditional masses, ceremonies are often kept short, with one or two readings included. Think about your guests' comfort with a long ceremony, especially if your wedding season is likely to have very hot or cold weather occurring. You don't want your guests baking in the sun while your endless ceremony plods along with too many readings, a few musical performances, and other lengthy rites. Pick your favorites, and save the other contenders for inclusion in your wedding program or—I love this idea!—on signs you'll use for décor around your wedding sites.

Vows

Your vows, too, can incorporate your destination wedding's beauty, as you write your own words to be spoken in promise to one another. You might, for instance, say that this gorgeous setting pales in comparison to your partner's beauty, and just as you all stand in awe at the endless horizon we see here, you stand in awe at the future that extends ahead of the two of you in your new life together. You get the picture.

Another way to "destination wedding up" your vows is to include a line or two in the language spoken by locals, using a wonderful phrase of that culture within your vows to one another.

Of course, your wedding vows don't have to be colored by your destination wedding location, or the culture. They can be purely your words, from a traditional script or written by the two of you, with focus only on the promises you make to one another and the appreciation you feel for one another. There's something to be said for too much insertion of your destination wedding location and traditions. If you have lots of local color and culture in your wedding and reception overall, you're free to keep your vows pure and simple, an undiluted message at the heart of your ceremony.

Here are some tips for your vows:

+ *Don't put pressure on yourselves to memorize them.* Your officiant can read them line by line from your cards, or you can read from your own cards. You may be nervous during your ceremony, which can cause the mind to blank and that precious moment to be tarnished.

- *Breathe.* Take your time, unlock your knees, breathe deeply, and relax so that you can read your vows more calmly.
- *Speak slowly.* When nervous, you might have a tendency to talk faster, which can lead you to trip over your words. Look into your partner's eyes and deliver each line of your vows with delicacy.
- *If you'll be joining families, take vows with the kids as well.* Promise to love and support them, sharing how proud you are of them. Don't pressure the kids to recite vows (unless they want to!). Just let them take in the love of that moment without any anxiety about talking in front of all of your guests.
- *Print your vows in your wedding program.* If you wish, let guests see the love within those vows, the beauty of your writing, and your love for one another.

Exchanging of Rings

Look into your destination wedding's traditions regarding the exchanging of rings. Some cultures have beautiful, symbolic rituals for this, ones you might

Planning Tip

I love the idea of getting new, crafted ring boxes for your rings. These are often velvet-lined and color-coordinated to your wedding, not the branded ring boxes from your jeweler, and they let you take gorgeous ring photos with your flowers, on your invitations, and wherever your photographer may want to capture them. But in the moment of your ceremony, the rings emerge nestled in these pretty ring boxes for superior presentation. See TheMrsBox.com online for gorgeous ideas and inspiration.

not be aware of from your own ancestry. Now that you're in the land of your forebears, it can be fascinating for your guests and so very meaningful to you to bring in this unique twist on the ring exchange and the words spoken while doing so.

Religious and Cultural Elements

Here, too, are opportunities to infuse your destination wedding location, culture, and style into your wedding, as well as religious rituals that are important to you. It can be fascinating to see another culture's take on religious wedding elements, and when you meet with your religious officiant, it's important to ask for descriptions of them so that you're not surprised during your ceremony when a religious rite looks and feels entirely different from what you expected. The ritual may be the same, but it may be the wording the officiant uses that can throw you a bit. Definitely look into these details, because when your wedding is helmed by a religious officiant, they may do things their own way.

So how do you find out about cultural wedding ceremony rituals? There are plenty listed online to consider, such as walking through a Moongate in Bermuda

Planning Tip

When you find a cultural association tied to your own ancestry, get involved in the group! Attend their events and festivals, participate in social media conversations, and learn more about your cultures. It's terrific to join a new community for enrichment in your marriage, and membership has its privileges for so many cultural wedding ideas and items. I've seen cultural association members lend out their wedding items, and this is a terrific way to find authentic, talented musical performers and other experts who can enhance your wedding.

for luck, or the exchanging of leis during a Hawaiian wedding ceremony. Your wedding planner will also have a supply of ideas, and your local vendors may also be able to suggest cultural rituals—even in areas different from their own sphere of expertise, such as a photographer letting you know about a food exchange ritual or the exchanging of coins for prosperity during the ceremony. I also recommend checking in with national cultural associations (you can find these on Facebook) for their input on cultural wedding traditions. These groups comprise elders who may have personal experience with these traditions, as well as younger members who may have recently incorporated cultural traditions in their own weddings. They are a wellspring of information.

Toss-Its

Before you buy post-ceremony toss-its such as birdseed-filled cones and flower petals meant for showering you during your recessional, first check with your destination wedding ceremony venue to make sure your group would be allowed to use them. Many houses of worship, resorts, and private venues say no to post-ceremony toss-its, citing the cost of cleanup and safety risks as their reason. So get permission first before buying and planning.

If there is no such restriction, consider toss-its that tie into your location and wedding style. Flower petals work in any location, of course, but they look all the prettier when they coordinate with the tropical or local flowers used in your ceremony décor. In a city loft, streamers might fit the bill, easily swept up without any risk of birdseed getting in tile ridges or causing slipping hazards for guests in high heels. At a winter wedding, silvery confetti can evoke a snowy effect when showering down around you.

This is an element that can be skipped, with applause or song "showering" you as you walk back up the aisle. Some couples prefer not to bring such props on the plane with them, fearing high baggage fees, and others would rather use that element of the budget elsewhere.

Wedding Program

Throughout this section, I've suggested interesting things to add to your wedding program, for your guests' fascination and as a forever record of your ceremony. Let me help organize your ceremony program inclusions here:

- Your full names (since some guests will be friends of yours or your partner's and might not know)
- The wedding date
- The wedding ceremony location
- The elements of the ceremony, in order, including any welcome remarks by a chosen speaker or your officiant, readings by title and author plus the name of the person reading, musical selections by name and composer plus the name(s) of the performer(s), any hymns or selections that you'd like guests to participate in—you'll add a note inviting guests to sing out loud or repeat wording
- Any note about the setting, such as historical significance or why you chose it
- Notes about cultural or religious rituals, so that guests may understand and appreciate the meaning behind them
- The names of your officiant, parents, bridal party members, and other honored guests
- A note in remembrance of loved ones who have passed away
- A note at the end, thanking your guests for attending your wedding and for the love they have always shown you, plus a note of thanks to your parents and to others who have helped create your wedding and provided a lifetime of love and support to the two of you

13

Planning Your Reception

WHAT WILL YOUR celebration be like? You're the author of your post-ceremony party, and given that this is a destination wedding, you may choose to incorporate elements of your location to further personalize your cocktail party and reception. As with any wedding these days, you don't have to adhere to any sort of set way of doing things. Guests tend to expect variations from the norm when they're at a destination wedding, so you have a lot of freedom to plan your reception your way from start to finish. Would you like cultural dancers to perform at the start of your reception, treating guests to a show as well as a dinner? That's a fine idea, and one that many destination wedding couples choose to start their celebration with some extra Wow Factor. You're in this marvelous place that you've chosen because you love its style and culture, so why not bring the setting's rich artistic DNA into your party? Without some semblance of local flair and flavor, guests might wonder why they came all this way, if you're going to have a cookie cutter wedding that you could have had back home. So use this section to find ways to insert the local culture into any number of your reception elements.

Cocktail Party

First off, will you even have a traditional pre-dinner cocktail party? Some couples prefer the cocktail party as a whole, so they design a wedding that's all-cocktail party. Five hours of passed hors d'oeuvres, drink stations with signature drinks, a relaxed format with so many food options to choose from on buffet tables and at stations (and yes, desserts at the end). They might feel that everyone in their circle, including them, loves the cocktail party portion so much more than a sit-down dinner that can slow down the momentum of the party. So they choose to go All Cocktail Party, all night long. It's a wedding style that guests love as well.

Now let's get into the details about the cocktail party itself, no matter how long you've decided it will last.

Seating

You have many options when it comes to the seating for your cocktail party, and since you may be in a stunning location such as an outdoor terrace overlooking the ocean or mountains, it's smart to take advantage of the views (and perhaps the glorious weather outside, such a contrast to the snowy, icy, slushy weather back home if that fits your wedding date). If your location can lend a gorgeous hand to

Don't Forget Your Guests

A cocktail party reception can be very pleasing to guests who have particular palates or specialty diet issues. When they have such a huge variety of dishes before them at the cocktail party, they have more to choose from. A sit-down dinner, by contrast, has just a handful of food options. So if you have many diets to consider and want your guests' cocktail party fare to go on and on, a cocktail party reception may be the right choice for you.

Watch Out!

Beware of often-reported wedding advice to have cocktail party seating for 30 percent or so of your guests, with the mind-set of guests mingling during the cocktail party. Everyone will want a place to sit down, set down their drinks and plates, and eat with ease. So be sure you have table seating for all, not just a portion of your guests. You don't want guests hovering over a table, awaiting (and pressuring) seated guests to leave so that they can snag the table. That's a feeling of mall food court or rest stop food court, not your fine wedding. Keep your guests ease and comfort in mind at all times.

your cocktail party setting, choose an area of your venue that lets your setting shine, as well as perhaps a dazzling sunset at the time of your cocktail party.

The setting you choose will help you design the seating for your cocktail party. The terrace may be long and on the narrow side, so one long table for the group may be an ideal seating plan in contrast with the larger ballroom or reception area that gives you many options for seating. You might opt to set several round tables around the cocktail party area, and I always love the idea of adding tables of different sizes to accommodate groups, such as bistro tables for couples who wish to sit alone, not knowing (yet) many of their fellow guests, and larger square or rectangular tables for larger groups of friends or family.

Décor

Your cocktail party gives you the chance to style two party settings, perhaps using a décor plan that you may have considered for your reception space but ultimately went another way. So let's say you wanted an authentic Hawaiian setting with lots of palm fronds and tropical flowers, shells and other islandy décor pieces, but for your reception opted for a more formal, elegant décor style for your ballroom. Your cocktail party setting gives you the perfect opportunity to theme your cocktail party space. But rather than it looking like a party supply store's Aloha section, you'll give those classic Hawaiian décor pieces some creative styling, perhaps with some DIY projects, Etsy artists' best work, and a blend of luau and formal party. You'll just turn the dial more to luau for this party, perhaps even having it on the beach, as your first stop before guests progress to your formal tented setting.

The key to cocktail party décor is looking at each theme décor piece, and deciding how to use it. Following the current repurposing trend, you might take a simple item such as a wood pallet and turn it into a bar. Or you might pile up vintage suitcases to create a unique, themed party station. A long piece of driftwood becomes a table runner, upon which flowers and candles are set. Infusing a themed décor piece into a larger, eye-catching décor statement is so much more fascinating than scattering starfish on a tablecloth (although you could certainly do that). Add plenty of votive candles and lanterns to elevate your décor with light, and your cocktail party setting glows with the prettiness of your chosen décor pieces.

Some décor ideas for your cocktail party that work into your destination wedding's location and style include:

- Signs, perhaps written with cultural styling, such as with classic Greek lettering, sharing quotes, song lyrics, or food and drink IDs for dishes with which guests might not be familiar
- Local florals and greenery
- Candles and lanterns

Budget Tip

Of course, you might opt to go minimalistic with décor for your cocktail party, leaving the Wow Factor décor items for your reception space. Depending upon your location, existing tropical floral trees and lighting effects already in place at your venue, a roaring fireplace, or small florals at each guest table (already provided by your venue) give your party space subtle décor that's friendly to your budget. Often, free.

- Arches and suspended florals
- Crystals everywhere, as well as frosted glass décor for a wintry look
- Nautical décor to suit your cruise or yacht wedding's style
- Tablecloths with cultural patterns on them, a favorite of mine for conveying your location and wedding style

Rentals

Talk with your wedding planner to find reputable rental agencies at your destination wedding location, since many of your rental items will be large and heavy. Boxes of linens can weigh a lot, for instance. These are not items to ship to your location. When it comes to a destination wedding in another country or on an island where cultural items may play a part in your décor dreams, a rented cultural item can add so much to your wedding's international flair. Consider the following types of rented items:

- Tables
- Chairs
- Linens
- Arch, trellis, or chuppah
- Pedestals
- Furniture
- Serving carts or trolleys
- Lighting, for illuminating the space
- Fans or heaters (not decorative, but essential, depending upon your location)
- Stages and flooring
- Curtains and décor linens
- Specialty plates
- Specialty glasses
- Specialty serving sets like sushi plates
- Chafing dishes, as needed

- Serving utensils
- And more…

Menu

Just a brief note to remind you that the menu for your cocktail party will ideally consist of a blend of cocktail party classics that guests love, plus a number of authentically created local dishes, giving your guests a taste of the local cuisine. Talk to your catering manager about the perfect combination of fresh bites and crunchy tastes, creating a sensory orchestration of your menu to suit all palates, in addition to loading up on gluten-free, vegetarian, vegan, and other dishes you know your guests prefer. Gorgeous displays will bring your cocktail party menu to life, and smartly planned stations keep lines from forming throughout your party space.

Bar

While open bar will always be a Must for any wedding, it's especially important for a destination wedding. When guests have spent a lot to get to a faraway wedding, you don't want them to pay for their drinks at the wedding. That's a giant Don't.

You might opt to create a different bar for your cocktail party—perhaps a bar at which specialty drinks are planned to pair with the dishes in the cocktail party menu. So, you might have a vodka bar, or a rum bar, in addition to your regular bar. Signature drinks may be served at this bar, and for added cocktail appeal, the signature drinks served here at this stage of the party may be different from the signature drinks you plan for your reception.

Pretty signage for your bar menu adds creative flair to your cocktail party as well, and for any local or specialty drinks, why not put on display drink recipe cards for guests to take home so that they can recreate your fabulous cocktails at their own parties?

Entertainment

It's always a good idea to arrange for entertainment at your cocktail party, to set the tone and again, add some local culture and seasonal flair to your celebration. Or, if you'd prefer to go classic for this party, hire a guitarist or pianist for softer tones and a romantic feel before your reception lights up with electronic dance music and potentially a cultural dance performance or band. Remember that the music creates a feeling, so think about how you'd like your guests to feel at your cocktail party. There's no rule saying you must keep the music on the softer, slower side. The choice is entirely up to you. Some couples like to plan for softer, slower music during the dinner hour, so you can certainly choose entertainment for your cocktail party that creates a certain sense of energy.

Reception

If you will have a traditional reception, complete with sit-down dinner and dancing, find ways to incorporate your personalities and your destination wedding setting, style, and culture into your plans. You know the celebration style of your group. Some people will stay on the dance floor and at the bar all night long, and some are quite content to stay at their tables with friends and family, taking in the scene, indulging in your menu and drink offerings, low-key but oh-so-happy to be there. Since you'll always keep your guests' comfort levels in mind, you'll focus on finding ways to make each of these groups satisfied beyond their expectations.

Seating

The size and shape of your tables are more than layout factors. You'll decide on classic twelve-seater tables versus long, all-inclusive tables for thirty to forty depending upon what you think, and what you've found at other events you've attended, will best facilitate your guests' togetherness factor. Do you prefer to gather everyone together at one long table, or do you think your guest list splits up into natural groups of ten to twelve? And does it even matter to you? You may find that it doesn't matter where you seat guests…they tend to get up and mingle throughout the reception, table-hopping and gathering at the bar or out on a scenic terrace anyway.

The trend has been to do away with splitting seating by sides of the family, what they used to call His Side and Her Side (although that wording has gone out the window lately). Now, guests are seated by what we can call Energy Level, their penchant for socializing, those who ditch their tables for the dance floor, and those who use their tables as their home base. So you might seat all of your friends together, all of your cousins on both sides, all of your older relatives together (far from the speakers), and so on. Kids will sit with their parents for better supervision, and bridal party members find it ideal to sit with their dates, spouses, and friends rather than at a head table for the bridal party. Again, completely up to you.

Décor

You know what you love for your reception décor, from low-set centerpieces to help facilitate conversation at your guests' tables (and not block their views), to tall, dramatic centerpieces adding Wow Factor to your reception space. For scope and size, the choice is always yours, and at many destination wedding locations, your setting has its own bounty of floral and foliage beauty to coordinate with. Some settings won't require you to decorate much at all, since Mother Nature has done all of the decorating for you, and some settings are blank canvases awaiting your design "paint brush."

Since you likely won't want to design décor that could be done anywhere, such as in your own hometown, you'll want to incorporate some of the local flair, florals, and style into your accents. Your wedding planner and floral designer will be of the utmost help in this, showing you images of locally inspired designs, likely from some weddings they've planned at your location. Check out those site-specific arrangements, garlands, potted trees brought in to transform your room and out-door spaces, and take notes on what you'd like to emulate, as well as what you may like to improve upon. The types of flowers in season at the time of your wedding will likely play a large part in your décor, and when you understand the rigors of importing blooms and greenery, as well as market shifts that can make some florals unavailable to your location, you can fine-tune your décor plan.

It's all about coordinating your larger, Wow Factor décor pieces with a myriad of smaller, complementary décor choices. Some of the best beauty is in the smallest

---

Planning Tip

No matter where your destination wedding will take place—exotic overseas country, island, or a state—that location has its own official flower. Here are some of the official flowers of several nations and islands:

ANTIGUA AND BARBUDA: *Dagger log*

ARGENTINA: *Seibo*

AUSTRALIA: *Golden wattle* (Australia has several different state flowers to consider)

THE BAHAMAS: *Yellow elder*

BARBADOS: *Pride of Barbados*

BELIZE: *Black orchid*

BOLIVIA: *Kantuta* and *Patuju*

BRAZIL: *Tabebuia alba*

CANADA: *Maple leaf* (and many provinces claim their own emblem flowers, such as the mayflower, the emblem of Nova Scotia)

PEOPLE'S REPUBLIC OF CHINA: *Peony, plum blossom, and chrysanthemum*

COLOMBIA: *Cattleya orchid*

DENMARK: *Red clover*

DOMINICAN REPUBLIC: *Mahogany tree flower*

EGYPT: *Lady's slipper*

FINLAND: *Lily of the valley*

FRANCE: *Fleur-de-lis* (iris)

GERMANY: *Cornflower*

GREECE: *Violet* and *laurel branch*

REPUBLIC OF INDIA: *Lotus*

IRELAND: *Shamrock*

ISRAEL: *Cyclamen*

ITALY: *Cyclamen*

JAMAICA: *Lignum vitae*

JAPAN: *Cherry blossom* (not actually official, but the bloom of choice)

JORDAN: *Black iris*

LAOS: *Plumeria*

MALAYSIA: *Chinese hibiscus*

details, like a tiny floral ring around the base of pillar candles, created from delicate flowers native to your wedding's location. When placed on guest tables, guests get a close-up look at this lovely little touch, multiplying the effect for your budget. A $2 floral ring can impress as much as a $200 floral centerpiece. So think like a floral designer, with equal attention to small and large accenting.

And don't forget the effects of gorgeous lighting, from color washes to up-lighting, to gobo lights custom-made to project your names or a cultural welcome message onto your tent, building, dance floor, entryway, or even onto your bar or

MALDIVES: *Pink rose*

MEXICO: *Dahlia*

NETHERLANDS: *Tulip*

NEW ZEALAND: *Silver fern*

NORTH KOREA: *Magnolia*

NORWAY: *Heather*

PERU: *Cantuta*

POLAND: *Corn poppy*

PORTUGAL: *Lavender, sunflower, red oak,* and *carnation*

RUSSIA: *Chamomile*

ST. KITTS AND ST. NEVIS: *Red royal poinciana*

SOUTH AFRICA: *King Protea*

SOUTH KOREA: *Hibiscus syriacus* (rose of Sharon)

SPAIN: *Carnation*

TAIWAN: *Plum blossom*

TRINIDAD AND TOBAGO: *Chaconia*

UKRAINE: *Sunflower*

UNITED KINGDOM: *Tudor rose* or *red rose* (each region has its own emblem flower, including the Welsh daffodil and the Scottish bluebell, among others)

URUGUAY: *Ceibo*

VENEZUELA: *Cattleya orchid*

VIETNAM: *Red lotus*

Be aware that many countries' regions claim their own individual flowers, and that some countries haven't yet decided on specific flowers to call their own. And while legislation was put into place in 1986 naming the rose as the official flower of the United States, each individual state—and each individual Hawaiian island!—claims its own official flower. This is an easy Google to help you select official flowers of your location, and you may wish to go beyond your wedding's location to choose the official flowers of your own heritages as a way to personalize your floral décor.

Yes, states have their own flowers as well, another easy Google to snag those pretty blooms of your stateside destination wedding location.

any flat surface ideal for sharing an illuminated message. Make room in your budget for lighting effects indoors and out, since they go a long way in transforming your site and elevating the beauty of all of your wedding décor.

Go beyond the obvious décor pieces, again, incorporating those shells and starfish into larger décor creations so that they don't look like a pre-school craft project but instead stand out as ingenious décor touches.

Rentals

The site you choose will likely help determine what needs to be rented for your wedding, and your wedding planner is a crucial part in making sure all of the most often-forgotten rentals are covered. You'll need rentals to guard your guests from the elements and temperature, such as fans, air conditioners, and surprisingly elegant mosquito nets where needed. Functionally, extra power supply may need to be rented, as will speakers and stages, as well as serving pieces to facilitate the loveliest serving of your menu items.

I see a lot of destination wedding couples renting extra portable bars, knowing that their site's one stationary bar will just not cut it for their group and for their plans for specialty bars.

I also see more rentals of photo booths to provide extra fun at the reception. Talk to your planner, your on-site event manager, and each of your local vendors to help build your full rental list. Your caterer might need some extra rentals that are on you to provide, and your entertainers can enlighten you about the flooring they need you to arrange that isn't in place at your venue. Getting a complete list of functional and decorative rental needs early saves you from last-minute frantic searching and expensive rush orders.

Your Entrance

If you have access to cultural dancers, drummers, or other exciting entertainers, make your grand entrance extra-special by having them precede or escort you into your reception for the grandest entrance possible. Make good use of this big moment by sharing the star power of your entrance with culturally authentic, colorful, and energetic performers guiding your way. It'll be an unforgettable moment. Or, if you'd rather not be joined in your walk, your band or deejay can play a local-styled song as your entrance music, also letting your location shine through your wedding plans.

Since a destination wedding can be unconventional, ask a friend to deejay your grand entrance, and some couples will also give their parents the honors if the parents have not had much of a part in the planning, and this would be a great moment for them.

One option is to play your "us through time" video before your entrance into the room, sharing all of those great photos of your baby portraits and dating days with your guests, a traditional entrance moment that culminates in your appearance.

Or simply just dance into the room, joining your bridal party in a choreographed number, or perhaps dancing with your local cultural performers for a high-energy entrance.

Find out if your location's culture has a time-honored tradition of presenting the wedding couple. You might love the ritual, if it isn't your family's practice already, of having a family elder present you with good-luck bread, wine, and salt as you start your married life with the traditional blessings. Or, your location's culture may have other symbolic gifts for you that add extra meaning to your marriage's fortuitous beginning.

Menu

You'll choose your menu with the help of your caterer and wedding planner, remembering to include several cultural dishes . . . or tweaks on authentic cultural dishes that may make them more palatable to your guests. Some cultures' traditional dishes can be surprising and a bit too out-there for your guests, so a substitution or crowd-friendly adjustment can be made. Of course, a completely classic menu of favorites that guests always enjoy at weddings may balance all of the unusual elements you're incorporating in your day, something that guests say they welcome. They're game to try some new tastes, in food and in drink, but when they're given superbly cooked classics, they have something to enjoy with comfort and ease. Not everyone is an adventurous eater, so consider some traditional menu options to ensure all of your guests are pleased. If your venue gives them three dinner options, make one adventurous and the other two classics.

Or, make your entrées classic for your guests' familiarity, and include an adventurous course in the middle.

Service Style and Servers

Find out what the local culture prefers when it comes to service style. Family-style dinners, which have guest tables presented with platters and tureens of food from which they help themselves, is a popular style globally as well as in current wedding trends you've seen back home. Gueridon service is one type of service style that has servers preparing each guest's plate from a cart they roll up to the table, personalizing each guest's dishes in the moment.

If you opt for a buffet dinner, be sure that buffet line has in-place attendants who can do the serving and customizing, also making sure chafing dishes are full, and that platter presentations stay neat and orderly.

Bar and Signature Drinks

Just like with your menu, mix up classic and traditional drinks with cultural drinks, to allow your guests the chance to try new flavors and, if they'd like, switch to their "usual" drinks if those new tastes aren't to their liking. A wide variety of drink options is a hallmark of an indulgent wedding, and a treat for those who have traveled too far to be greeted with a wine and beer bar with no other options. You don't need to stock your bar with the priciest spirits and bubbly, but you do need to make sure that guest drink requests can be fulfilled.

First Dances

Your first dance as a married couple is one of those amazing Firsts that you'll always remember, and these days, many couples are hiring choreographers to help them make their first dance something special. While you could always slow-dance to your song, you may want to show off your moves with a sensational and riveting tango. Especially if your wedding takes place in the land where the tango was born. Incorporating a local dance style—even for just a part of your first dance—is a splendid way to pay homage to the location you've chosen, and incorporate the culture that becomes part of your wedding's DNA. You'll find an excellent variety of wedding dance choreographers online, and expand your search beyond "wedding dance" choreographers. Any number of talented, expert dance instructors

---

Planning Tip

During your scouting trip, you might choose to meet with a choreographer locally, to help you design an authentic, culturally focused special dance just for you. Videotape your lesson, so that you can practice when you're back home (which you would do with a lesson from a local-to-you choreographer).

can guide you in creating your first dance, and some couples seek out college-level, advanced dance students who can choreograph an authentic, cultural first dance.

Some couples start off with a traditional slow dance, then the music changes—a surprise to your guests—and you break into a new style of dance. The same can be done for father-daughter and mother-son dances, turning your parents' dances into something to behold as well, and a lot of fun for them . . . especially if they're not comfortable with a slow dance and would prefer something more lively.

I love the idea of asking grandparents to dance a short segment of Their Song, and if you're combining families, how about a group dance in which your kids join you? Add some extra excitement for the kids by having them help pick the song and help design the choreography. The result is a fabulous performance the kids will love, cheered by the applause of your guests. And there's always the chance in one of these group dances for spotlight moments for each of your kids. Maybe your tween child will get to do a drum solo (with permission of the band, of course), and your little ones can bang away on bongos. Their performance doesn't always have to be a dance.

Keep in mind that you can close your reception with a last dance for the two of you, another opportunity to pick a special song that means a lot to you. You start off the dance alone on the dance floor, then invite all of your guests to join you. And again, that romantic song can segue into a higher energy song with a great message, a fabulous end to your unforgettable celebration.

Special Moments for Others

You may wish to share the spotlight on your big day with a friend who wishes to pop the question to one of your relatives or friends in front of all loved ones. You adore them, so you don't mind. In a matter of good etiquette, the question-popper will ask for your permission ahead of time . . . always the way to go so as not to steal your spotlight and take advantage of all you've done to create a gorgeous setting. That's just bad wedding etiquette.

Planning Tip

If you'll make room in your plans for a guest's proposal or anniversary shout-out, let your venue manager and wedding planner know. Very often, the site can whip up a special cake or dessert for the people you'd like to honor.

It's become a new wave of kindness as more wedding couples are more than happy to allow their loved ones a gorgeous and very special moment, sharing their news about their pregnancies and engagements with all, and we're seeing a lot of birthday cake presentations to guests whose birthdays fall on or near the wedding date. With everyone gathered for your lovefest, this is a celebration moment that person wouldn't otherwise have. Milestone birthdays, milestone anniversaries, and other celebrations are being included in destination wedding plans in big numbers now, so think about whom you might fete with a surprise cake and a big announcement, a song dedication or a special gift.

Toasts/Blessing

If you'd like to open your reception with a prayer or blessing, your officiant—who should be invited to your reception as a matter of good etiquette—can do the honors. Or, you might choose a special family member or friend to do so. If your faith is important to you, this can be another way to incorporate your beliefs into your wedding celebration. And if you simply love the idea of your marriage, and your guests, being given a blessing, plan ahead of time for this segment of your celebration. Your officiant or loved one should have some advance notice of your request, so that a scripted blessing can be created by them for the ultimate in loveliness and wonderful sentimentality at the start of your reception.

Entertainment Moments

A destination wedding opens up many chances to do a little something different from what all of your guests have seen at other weddings. Cultural dances and musical performances can pop up at any time, giving guests a show and revving up the excitement level at your wedding. As mentioned, you might join in, or guests might be invited to join in as they are comfortable. You don't want your entertainment to come to a screeching halt in order for an act to be introduced. Your deejay or bandleader will make sure that a smooth transition happens, using their expertise in reception flow. This is another reason why you want to work with true professionals, skipping old and bad advice to ask friends and family members to "work" your wedding in any way. Assessing the crowd and knowing how the energy will flow in the room is an art form, one that the best entertainers have mastered.

Be open to their suggestions for your reception's big entertainment moments. They may suggest acts or presentations that you never thought of, and they may also do you the great favor of preventing you from overloading your entertainment moments, stopping and starting the energy of your celebration.

14

Pretty Little Details

Here is where your wedding artistry shines, in the smallest of details that convey so much of your personal style, your wedding's theme, your personalities, and the heart of your relationship. While I couldn't possibly prescribe design styles to you, what I will do here is share Top 5 trends and tips for each of the wonderful little details of your day.

Save-the-Date Cards and Invitations

1. Save the Dates should be mailed out to your official, final guest list people as far in advance as possible. It's part of your "thinking of your guests" consideration and etiquette to give them lots of time to block off days in their schedule, make their travel arrangements, get babysitters and pet sitters lined up, and get ready to attend your big day. Aim for at least twelve to sixteen

weeks in advance, according to "when to send" etiquette rules, but more realistically, if you can send Save the Dates out way sooner, at least six months in advance, that often works best and helps ensure your beloved guests can attend happily.

2. You don't have to choose a Save-the-Date card style that conveys your destination wedding location. If you fall in love with a classic, romantic style of STD, by all means, use that one. You don't have to feature palm trees on it for your island wedding. Guests will see your location printed on your Save the Date and envision those palm trees all by themselves.

3. Be sure your personal wedding website and gift registry are all set up before you send out your STDs, since guests are going to head right to the URL you provide to start making their plans and start shopping for you.

4. For your invitations, you can use formal, etiquette-prescribed wording, or go more informally as you wish. Just be sure to include dress code information at the bottom of your card, such as "Formal attire" or "Island casual" so that guests know what to expect. I love the idea of putting dress code details more fully on your personal wedding website, such as "Rehearsal dinner will be formal" and "Pack your swimsuit and cover-up for our snorkeling adventure and yacht party."

5. Send invitations way in advance as possible, at least twelve to sixteen weeks in advance.

Menu Cards

1. Place one printed menu card on each guest's plate, so that they get to read their own pretty card when they arrive at their seats, whetting their appetite for your fabulous menu choices.

2. A big trend in menu cards is to have a calligrapher write each guest's name on top of the card, personalizing it.

3. Menu cards are especially valuable if you'll include some local or cultural dishes that guests may not be familiar with. Work with your chef to describe menu courses in detail, so that guests know what to look forward to—or avoid if they have an allergy.
4. Include a line letting guests know that your venue offers specialty diet meal replacements, such as gluten-free. All they have to do is ask.
5. If you prefer, style one menu card in a frame or affixed to a solid backing to display on each guest table.

Seating Cards

1. First things first: proper etiquette. Spell all guests' names correctly, and get the names of any guests' dates so that they see their names on the card as well.
2. Think about saving paper while you convey your setting, theme, and style with a unique place card choice. Write guests' names on shells, sea glass, stones, wine corks, or other scene-connected mini items.
3. Go vertical with place card displays, affixing cards to stand-up shutters or jute, ribbon, or other strings upon which cards are clipped.
4. Skip cards altogether, and write guests' names and table numbers on a large mirror or glass pane window put on display.
5. *Do* arrange a seating plan. Some guests get anxious about finding seats when there is no seating assignment for them.

Itineraries

1. Include in each guest's welcome basket a printed itinerary sharing the details of all of the weekend's social events, so that they know where to

be at what time, and also which blocks of time they have "off" for their own socializing and relaxing.

2. Provide a contact number for guests to use if they have questions about events. If your wedding planner is okay with it, you may provide his or her number or e-mail for this.

3. Include on your itineraries the hotel's free Wi-Fi code, if available. Guests *love* getting this detail before they rack up huge roaming charges.

4. Provide dress code information for all events.

5. Provide costs that guests will be expected to pay at the event, such as for a group kayak trip at $20 per person, so they know to bring some cash with them.

Signs

1. Add some personality to your wedding display signs, with a touch of humor and sayings that mean a lot to your friends and family. Romantic quotes are always a great touch, and can come home with you to become décor in your house.

2. Signs can be weighty and unwieldy to bring on the plane, so these would be something to ship to your location. It won't be much of a savings, but it's a smart way to get those signs there reliably.

3. Create signs for unexpected places, like in the restroom and at your welcome cocktail party.

4. Include the local language in your signs, getting a knowledgeable translator to help you so that your sign doesn't elicit the wrong reaction with incorrect wording or grammar.

5. Consider fabric banner signs to make shipping or carrying in easier and cheaper, allowing you the personalization of signs without so much expense and trouble packing.

Guest Book

1. A simple guest book will do, just a lined journal that can be purchased on the cheap at any craft store.
2. No need to assign someone to man the guest book. Let your guests enjoy the wedding and reception without having to work.
3. Offer pens that work with your wedding colors. Guests love getting creative with multiple pen colors. You may get some stellar original artwork in your guest book.
4. If you'd like, skip the guest book. You'll have guests' wedding cards as keepsakes.
5. Instead of a guest book, have guests sign wine corks at your winery wedding or sea glass, stones, or shaped cards and then drop them into a glass vase or centerpiece bowl.

Family Photos

1. Bring *copies* of valuable family photos so that important treasures are not lost or damaged.
2. Match your family photos to your destination wedding location, such as snowy winter photos, beachy photos, lakeside photos, to suit your theme and décor, and also show off photos that tell a story about why this setting is important to you.
3. Add captions and ID signs to photos, sharing with guests who is in the photos and which events they're from. Add some color and theme-matching motifs to your ID cards to coordinate with the room.
4. Include in your family photos collection those professional photos you had taken here at your destination wedding locale, or make a display of *just* the photos from that shoot for your own separate couple's photo display.

5. If anyone in your family has a connection to your destination wedding location, share that story in your ID signs. This may be the town where your great-grandparents were married. Your guests will delight in knowing that *and* seeing that in their wedding photos.

Comfort Items

1. In cold weather climate locations, *or if the weather reports are calling for cooler than usual temperatures in a usually hot location,* set out a basket of pashminas for guests to wrap themselves in.
2. In hot weather locations, set out a basket of sunscreen and damp washcloths set on ice, for sun protection and cooling.
3. In hot and humid weather, many venues will send out a server with a tray of ice water for guests' hydration as well. Or they'll set up ice water decanters in easy reach of guests.
4. Create a site-specific amenities basket in the restroom, with itch-relieving insect bite sticks for those mosquito bites, plus mosquito repellent, sunblock lip balm (for cold and hot weather locations!), and antacids if the local cuisine is spicy.
5. Include in your amenities basket blister pads to help guests whose shoes may be rubbing the backs of their feet. When shoes are worn from a sandy setting into an indoor room, some of that grit can create irritation to feet. Guests will appreciate this thoughtful comfort item.

15

Legalities

As GORGEOUS AS your wedding is going to be with all of your large and small details, you've got to make your marriage legal. The fascinating and frustrating thing about destination weddings is that every location across the globe has its own laws and rules about marriage licenses, waiting periods, blood tests, witnesses, and other requirements needed to be proven and provided before your destination wedding ceremony can make your marriage legal. There's not just one rule across the board out there. Every country, every island, has its own marriage license and permissions rules, and in some countries, the rules vary from town to town. Some locations require you to be present in their country or on their island—for "residency" to be established—anywhere from a day to six months. I'm sure there's some tiny municipality or island out there that has a rule longer than six months.

Bottom line: there are a ton of rules regarding destination weddings and marriage licenses in so many locations across the world, and your decision to marry away means you're right in the middle of these rules, having to find out which rules are current and which are outdated, then making your scouting visit plans to coincide with license applications in correct timing to make sure your marriage license will still be active and valid when you marry. It can make your head spin.

Luckily, you have an experienced, professional wedding coordinator who knows how to navigate the minefield of legalities for your destination wedding's location, and can help you with each step, including the one step that surprises a lot of couples:

Where to Find Your Location's Marriage License Rules

It's research time! Destination weddings have a few extra steps not usually found in planning an at-home wedding, but this is not one of them. No matter where you're planning to marry—even if it's a country club a few towns over or your own backyard—you'll need to research the marriage license rules for where your wedding will take place. There's no one rule for domestic weddings, just as there's no one rule for any overseas location. (And let's not forget that your destination wedding may be at a domestic location!)

For a domestic wedding, you'll check on the marriage license rules at the town hall where your wedding will take place. For an international wedding, you'll check with any of the following:

- *The tourism board at that location.* Check 360travelguide.com/tourist.asp or State.gov for lists of world tourism office locations, noting that some countries—like Greece, for instance—have many different tourism offices listed by city or town, so you'll need to be extra cautious about contacting the right one. In some regions, the city where your wedding will take place is actually a different city from what you might expect. So this is a double-check situation.
- *The consulate or embassy at that location.* Many will have their current marriage license information posted on their website, *but* call for details just to be sure. Just like some websites haven't been updated in a while, and since laws change every day, you don't want to operate under outdated information. Take that website list as your first research step, then confirm it with an officer at the embassy.
- *Your wedding planner.* Whether it's the planner on-site or your local planner—or both!—they can research the marriage license rules for you and potentially get extra, useful information like the best time of day to go for your license or to appear before a magistrate. Let's say the registrar's office closes at 3:00 p.m. local time, and you've planned your site visit for an

Planning Tip

Make an appointment for your marriage license application. Some offices say that walk-ins are fine, but you could be sitting there for hours. An appointment might not get you in the door at exactly the time you book, but it is likely to help prevent an all-day wait.

afternoon trip to the registrar. This inside information can save you time and money, and potentially save your scouting trip itinerary.

Want to make sure your marriage will be considered legal at home? Check with the attorney general's office in your home state for rules and requirements.

Which Documents Will You Need?

Your location's tourism site or marriage license website will list the documents you'll need to bring with you, and again, call to be sure you have everything that is required. Here are some documents you'll likely need to have on hand, depending on the site's requirements:

- *Your passports.* And make sure they're current. Some locations require a copy of your last two passport stamps.
- *Your photo IDs.* Some locations require at least two forms of photo ID.
- *Your birth certificates.* Most sites that require them will want to see original copies, and some locations require you to have them translated into the local language, using one of their official translators. That's going to cost you.

Planning Tip

That's not all of the documentation you'll need. While the above relates to your marriage license, you may need documents required by the house of worship in which you plan to marry. They may need to see copies of your baptism records and certification that you've taken the required pre-marriage religious course. Ask your officiant for a list of all documents you'll need. If you find that you don't qualify for a religious wedding ceremony, you may be able to get a "blessing ceremony" instead.

- *Divorce papers.* These documents are necessary if either or both of you have been divorced.
- *Death certificates.* Some locations may require documentation if either or both of you have been widowed.
- *Blood test results.* Check to see if you have to have blood tests done there, or if you can bring results of blood tests conducted at home. Timing is a big factor here, since you'll need the proper number of days for your blood test appointment and for your results to come in. Not every location has results within minutes or hours.
- *Miscellaneous.* Check to see what other documents may be required by the marriage license office.

Residency Rules

This is a big deal, so pay special attention to your location's residency rules. By "residency," they mean how long you need to be physically in the location before you can marry there legally. Some locations just need you to be there the day before—and they call that residency—and some need you to be there for weeks or months prior to your wedding. Some need at least one of you to be an actual citizen of the country or island. I've seen some locations' marriage license rules lists and found that residency affects prices by a lot. If one partner has citizenship in the country and the other does not, it costs more than if both of you were citizens. If neither of you have actual citizenship, it will cost you more.

This is the complicated stuff that can cause some couples to opt for getting legally married before their destination wedding—tying the knot at a civil or religious ceremony to be officially married—and then, not needing to get a license in-country, they have a "symbolic" wedding ceremony at their destination wedding, with the reception to follow. No paperwork needed, and no worrying if their marriage will be considered legal back home. You'll see the term "symbolic wedding" on many websites, and that's what it's referring to, not a wedding with lots of symbolism in it. A common misconception, one that causes problems for couples who proceed without a wedding planner or solid research. (Keep in mind that some locations don't allow symbolic weddings. They'll only perform "the real deal." Again, a wedding coordinator can let you know about that.)

So know the residency requirements before you book your flight, and make sure you're getting yourselves to your location in plenty of time to fulfill that rule.

Your wedding planner will be able to help you navigate the rules of your marriage license, and many will help with the process of applications and completion.

Witnesses

Some locations require a certain number of witnesses for the application and signing of your marriage licenses, and some may say that relatives are needed, or that your witnesses can't be your relatives. So be sure you know the rules and have the right people to bring along with you.

Can You Just E-mail Your Papers?

They never make it easy. While it may seem logical and efficient to just e-mail your documents to the registrar's office, most locations require you to apply in person. And some will require you to appear before a judge or magistrate for your permissions and signed documents. Work that process into your schedule.

Waiting Periods

Complicating things further, potentially, is each location's waiting period rule. You may have to wait two or three days after a marriage license is issued to be able to marry, for the license to be valid. You may have to wait a week. And conversely, your license may be good for only two or three days, meaning you have to get married within that time period. You've got to know your dates and plan accordingly.

One timing rule that trips up many couples is the location's waiting period after a divorce. They may say that you have to wait ten months to a year after your divorce is official to be granted a marriage license with them. Some spots around the world don't have this waiting period, but it's essential to know what the rule is if one or both of you have been divorced. The same goes for widows and widowers. The location may have a waiting period for you, too.

Speaking of timing, be sure to arrive at your wedding destination a few days prior to your big day, to allow time for last-minute documents to be handled, your license acquired, and any fixes made in time.

Getting Married Before Your Destination Wedding...Or After

I mentioned earlier that some couples, wanting to get married in their dream location but unwilling or unable to fulfill that long list of rules and requirements for a marriage license issued there, decide to get married officially before their destination wedding. They just don't want to jump through all of those hoops. They might just go to city hall to tie the knot officially and have their wedding in their destination wedding location later. They may or may not let people know they've done so, to cut back on guests' questions and potential annoyance at being "made" to go to a faraway location because the wedding couple wants to have a wedding "someplace pretty." Folks can be cranky like that. So it's up to you if you'd like to keep your "we made it official" news to yourselves.

You would then have a symbolic wedding at your destination wedding location, but the feelings are all the same. This is when you appear before your partner in your gown, walk down the aisle to authentic regional music, take your vows, and celebrate in style. This is your wedding, and many couples consider that date

Planning Tip

If you do decide to get married officially before your destination wedding, don't change your name right away. Your name has to be the same as the one on your passport and plane tickets in order for you to travel.

to be the anniversary they celebrate, no matter what the official date on their license says. Some couples celebrate two anniversaries, one for their civil ceremony and one for their destination wedding date.

Another option is to have your symbolic destination wedding, then marry officially afterward. This might be the option if you thought all of your paperwork was in order for your destination wedding, but it turned out not to be so. Or, it might be your original plan, without any paperwork nightmare forcing you into this choice. After your symbolic wedding at your destination, without a valid, signed marriage license in hand, you can then marry officially at home. One idea to consider is having your symbolic wedding take place at your destination wedding location, then get officially married (as a surprise to guests) at your hometown post-wedding celebration.

Additional Legalities

Check your passports right now to be sure you have plenty of time for them to be valid. If you'll need to apply for passports, or renew them, do that as far in advance as possible. Some wedding couples have found that the locations where they can apply for passports have changed, and they now have to make plans to travel farther. Or, they find out frighteningly late that their passports are expired, and they have to pay rush fees to get new ones issued and sent to them.

You may find that some destinations say that passports aren't required for entry, but you never know where your flight might get diverted to, so bring yours along anyway. Some destinations don't need a passport for entry, but—oddly—you need one to get home. Beat the system and get peace of mind by making sure you have valid passports.

Also, consider travel and wedding insurance, to cover you for a number of wedding-wrecking catastrophes. Any destination wedding location can experience its own weather event, and any venue can have a mishap. Look at reputable sources of insurance, and read all of the fine print, to be sure you understand what

Thinking of Your Guests

Include on your personal wedding website information about passports for your guests. You don't want any of them to experience travel hassles or impossibilities because they didn't know they needed a passport, or if a diversion sends them somewhere where they do need them. Consider this wording: "Even though our destination doesn't require passports for travelers, we advise bringing your valid passports along just to be safe."

is and isn't covered in case of damage, non-service, non-appearance, cancellation, rescheduling, and other issues that can—if not covered—impact your wedding and potentially cost you thousands of dollars.

Nothing mentioned in this chapter is to be taken as legal advice. I recommend you connect with an attorney for all of your legal concerns, as well as to create wills and other documents after the wedding.

That said, and as a reminder that this is the legalities chapter, get everything in writing, and keep it all organized.

16

Your Scouting Visit

TAKING A SCOUTING visit to your destination wedding resort or venue gives you many big advantages in planning your dream getaway wedding. There's no substitute for actually standing on the beach where you will someday take your wedding vows. A pretty photo online doesn't capture the feeling of that spot entirely, and that photo may have conveniently cropped out the outdoor party deck of a nearby restaurant, sure to cause privacy and noise issues on your wedding day. Photos online may be outdated, with new condos built in what would be your view of the mountains. Online photos are styled to make the place look perfect. What you see during your scouting visit can tell another story, and save your wedding when you can then say, "We'd like to pick another spot on the grounds." From views to sounds to smells, like the sickening aroma of fish from the docks to the scents of cooking from a nearby restaurant, you'll get to give your venue a test drive in a sensory way.

Checking Out the Setting

Try to schedule your scouting visit for the same season when your wedding will take place, if you have the time and ability to travel there a full year prior to your big day. You can then see what the venue looks like when it's in bloom in, say, spring. You can also spot dry, crunchy, brown grass where the website showed bright green lawn for your ceremony spot, the "usual" appearance of the grounds during drought season. Now, I say this with full understanding that a drought can happen at any time of year, and the one before you now might be an aberration. But it's something you can ask your on-site wedding planner about, so that you know if drought is the norm during this time of year or if it's just been an unseasonably dry time. You might also be told about the resort's new sprinkler system going in next month that will help ensure greener grass on your wedding day. While no one can make promises about the weather and about a lawn's appearance, it's good to see it in person and to ask questions.

Also thinking about the environment, how do your allergies feel when you're in your future wedding spot? Some people have sensitivities to certain kinds of flowers, plants, pollen, and molds, and if you're not used to that region's air quality or allergens, you might wish to take action for your own allergy treatments so that you're less likely to be red-eyed, sniffly, stuffed-up, and lethargic. Again, you're feeling your location during this scouting trip, taking everything into consideration. It may be too late to cancel your wedding, for fear of loss of deposit, but changes in location likely can be made this far in advance.

Even without any problems at your chosen wedding location, you might still spot an even more amazing setting for your ceremony or reception, and again, with this much advance notice, you may be able to change your sites if they aren't booked already.

During your scouting visit, ask to see venues for your other wedding events, such as your welcome cocktail party, rehearsal dinner, wedding morning breakfast, after-party, and morning-after breakfast, as well as locations for the events you'd like to plan for your wedding weekend. You may be able to book the restaurant, the sugar mill ruins, or another gorgeous site before another wedding couple or group does.

You also may wish to venture out into the town near your venue, checking out restaurants, bars, and shopping areas that might become part of your wedding weekend plan. While you're venturing, look for good-to-know places like coffee shops and pharmacies for your guests' information.

Meeting with Your Team

Now is when you finally meet face-to-face, after so many e-mails and perhaps a bunch of Skype sessions with your experts. You've built a long-distance relationship with your pros thus far, and now it's time to work together in person, with a great vibe for each other and an advantage in this not being a blind meeting work session.

Here are the wedding professionals you'll meet with:

- *Your wedding planner*. Review plans you've made thus far, and make any changes as you do a walk-through of your sites and a sit-down to discuss all of the next details to cover.
- *Your officiant*. This is a meeting that may be required by your location, and even if it's not required, it's a great idea to make an appointment to talk about what you'd like included in your ceremony as well as to find out what you can expect of the rituals within the ceremony. Again, you'll

Planning Tip

This is another reason to conduct your scouting trip a year before your wedding, in the same season as your wedding. The food you'll taste will be in-season, which can affect its flavors. Think about when you eat a watermelon in the middle of summer. It's crisp and juicy. When fall approaches, watermelon can get soft and grainy, depending upon where it's shipped from. It's out of season near you, and the taste just isn't the same. When you taste in-season foods that will be served at your wedding, you'll get the full flavor and texture as it will be on your big day.

get a sense of the officiant's personality, and create a connection that can add richness to your ceremony when he or she learns more about your relationship. You may also get a greater sense of trust in your officiant to help keep nerves away.

• *Your caterer.* If you haven't already picked out your menu for your reception, as well as your menus for other events like your rehearsal dinner and welcome cocktail party if you'll have all of these events in the same place, now's the time to enjoy this process. You'll be guided through the site's catering menus and enjoy a menu tasting to help you pick out your ideal dishes. If you'll have multiple events catered by different experts or restaurants, you'll attend meetings and tastings at each one, if available. Some restaurants don't do wedding tastings, so you may need to just go have dinner there to try out their cuisine.

• *Your cake baker.* You'll pick out flavors, if you haven't already. And here is the sweet awesomeness of getting to taste little squares or slices of so many different cake flavor combinations, as well as additional desserts if your cake baker will make them. This and the menu tasting are huge benefits that come from your scouting trip, something you couldn't possibly experience at a distance. And you might find, for baked goods as well as for desserts, that your location's version of a food you liked from the menu list isn't to your tasting, and may be made entirely differently in-country than what you're used to at home. Changes must be made!

- *Your bar manager.* In addition to planning your bar menu overall, for each of your events hosted at that location, you'll get to work with your mixologist to come up with and name your signature drinks. That's a tasting you'll enjoy as well.

- *Your floral designer.* Again, in-season, you'll see the types of flowers that may be used in your wedding décor, as well as for all of your events. You can work together, bringing up your Pinterest boards on your phone or on a tablet, to co-design all of your wedding florals and décor. Since you're there in their studio—and this is an advantage that many couples don't think about ahead of time—you may be able to check out any décor items your floral designer has available from prior weddings. Such as a driftwood table runner, or lanterns. These items may be rented, or may be added to your package for free, depending on your floral designer's preferences and the strength of your relationship.

- *Your wedding photographer.* This meeting, during which you'll tour your sites and talk about the shots and albums you want, could also turn into a photoshoot for the two of you. If you didn't get, or aren't happy with, your engagement photo session, now could be the perfect time to style and shoot some amazing photos of the two of you. You'll get to take advantage of the beauty of your setting and capture some truly lovely images that might also become part of your wedding's décor. Imagine that stunning

Budget Tip

When you're a joy to work with, you might get some extras thrown in for free.

sunset kiss shot enlarged and put on display at your ceremony's entrance, something you couldn't get if you hadn't visited your site in advance.

* *Your entertainers.* They might audition just for you, or you might be able to catch them in action at another event they have going on. When some couples go to see their musicians perform, the event they're at will often feature other performers, who they may love enough to hire as well, having seen their great show. Independent performers might not have an online presence, so there may have been no way to find them without being on-site.
* *The hotel concierge.* This is an often-missed opportunity. The hotel's concierge can give you information on booze cruises, festivals, group snorkeling or kayak outings, snow tubing outings, and other activities that can fill your wedding weekend activities list, and some resorts may grant wedding couples discounts on their bookings. If the resort has enough locations to fill your event wish list, you may never have to take everyone out into town for anything. No travel costs.
* *The beauty specialists.* Visit with your chosen hairstylist and makeup artist for your trial runs conducted by the people who will beautify you on your wedding day. Trial runs done at home can be a great idea to help you think about your best looks, but it's important to find out if your chosen stylists can do that updo, or maybe suggest something even prettier.

Staying in the Room

If your wedding hotel is very expensive, you might consider staying in a nearby, less expensive hotel and using that as your home base while you plan with your experts at your wedding hotel. That can be a smart idea for your budget, but you'd miss out on experiencing the hotel room at your wedding resort. It's a good idea to stay in a room at your venue, just to get a feel for the quality, how well room service performs, how quickly the bar cart gets to you, and especially what it's like

Planning Tip

Take photos as you go, and take plenty of notes during your scouting trip. As things get busier, you might forget about a special little detail or a question you had during this visit.

to move around the resort from your room. Some resorts are built on mountains and on volcanic islands, creating lots of hills to traverse and stairs to climb. Would your guests be able to handle such hiking, or is there a shuttle that circulates around the property, making it easier to get around? You find out more when you immerse yourself in the setting, and trying out a room is a great way to do this.

You also may be granted permission to tour the resort's suites, which can aid you in booking your own for the wedding weekend and allow you to make suggestions to your parents and bridal party (the latter perhaps, then deciding to share a suite, to cut down on individual costs!).

Order room service while you're there, and make note of any signs of disrepair. During your scouting visit, you can set up your hotel room block—if you haven't already—knowing better which suites, rooms, and villas may be to your and your guests' liking.

You'll also get a sense of the noise level at your hotel, since you may hear the pulsing music from someone else's wedding taking place across the resort, finding that the party then continues on to the beach where you're staying. You might not mind, but your guests might. Talk to your planner, then, about which rooms are located in the quieter sections of the resort, and arrange for more noise-sensitive guests like your parents (or you!) to be lodged there.

Part 3

Getaway Celebrations

THESE SEPARATE GETAWAY celebrations aren't parts of your destination wedding weekend. They're additional getaways with some of your favorite people, or just for the two of you. Now keep in mind that "getaway" doesn't always mean a far-away excursion with a plane ride needed. When you're planning a destination wedding that does require air travel, or trains or buses, it's a smart idea to choose a nearby destination that gives all of you a break on your travel budgets. When you consider that bridesmaids will spend over $1,000 on average to be in your wedding—including their dresses, shoes, the bridal shower, and gifts—a destination wedding can bump up their financial obligation to perhaps much more than that. Asking them, or groomsmen, to pay hundreds more for this extra trip you'd like them to attend is a dicey proposition. Especially since bridesmaids can feel that they have to attend a bachelorette getaway trip. There's no way to skip it, they might feel, and there they are again spending big money. That can make for cranky bridesmaids and friendship strife in the middle of your planning process.

So let's take a look at some great, budget-friendly girls' getaways and guys' getaways that keep good etiquette in mind and invite your nearest and dearest to a much-needed, much-appreciated vacation with just your close circle. Perhaps the way you used to vacation before life got busy for everyone, weddings and babies happened, and those annual beach or ski trips faded away. Even if you've only missed one summer or winter of your annual trips, this return to your carefree days can be most welcome for all.

17

Girls' Getaways

GIRLS' GETAWAYS ARE quickly taking the place of racy bachelorette parties, the ones with the male dancers, tons of alcohol, and X-rated décor and props. These raunchy parties used to be a Must, and were often planned by eager bridesmaids even when this type of party was so not the style of the bride. Grooms got possessive and renewed dislike for the bride's party-minded friends, and arguments often ensued. Drunk guests regretted their over-consumption the next day, or during the party, and someone always got stuck with a huge bar tab.

As time passed, and as the racy bachelorette party became less popular, a new kind of celebration just for the girls came to pass. The girls' getaway trip evolved from bachelorette parties that flew to Vegas and did the racy thing there. Now, girlfriend getaways are more likely to be pampering trips to spa resorts, a ski trip just for the ladies, a trip to wine country for more responsible drinking, or a shopping-centric trip to the big city.

Girls' getaways have a different agenda now: quality time with the girls, not quality time with a tequila bottle.

And photos from this girls' getaway can be shared on social media.

If you'd like to get away from it all—from your job, from wedding planning stress, from all of life's responsibilities—and just have a few fabulous days with your friends, a Girls' Getaway is for you. And for your friends, who may be weary of the bride version of you, of the topic of weddings and pairing up and wedding registries and picking out dresses. They want the return of the you they know, so that they can step out of their own world of "have to" and reconnect with their best friends again. You make that happen, for the benefit of all. And your friends won't have to worry about tensions in their relationships over the issue of a raunchy bachelorette party. It's a Win all the way around.

Girls' Getaway Styles

You'll see in this list of possible girls' getaway styles that flying isn't always needed, although some groups are fine with it since they have a ton of airline miles to use or they have the budget for a $70 airfare special. Again, if your destination wedding will require everyone to fly across the globe for your big day, a closer destination can be a fine choice to limit or eliminate high travel costs. A closer spot can also give you more time for togetherness, since you're traveling only an hour away, and the ability to use the entirety of your first and last getaway days for fun, not travel time. And a nearby spot with no air travel needed can also help some friends arrive the next day or leave a day early with ease, to get home for their responsibilities or for other social events they'll attend.

* Wine country getaway
* Fall leaf-peeping getaway
* Ski weekend
* Spa resort stay

- Attending a music festival
- Attending a food festival
- A weekend in a nearby big city, for theater, shopping, and dining
- A weekend in a quaint little tourist town, with a stay at a bed-and-breakfast or charming hotel
- A weekend at a nearby hotel, for downtime by the pool, hot tubbing, dining, and shopping
- A weekend at a camp that runs private stays and adult weekends, for a return to your childhood camping days—a getaway that's becoming more and more popular, and that some couples are choosing for their wedding weekend as a whole
- A weekend at a theme park, an entirely different experience with friends than it is when bringing kids, and some theme parks have fabulous restaurants and bars for grown-up time
- Camping, including glamping with decked-out tents and structures, gourmet dining and hiking guides, stargazing guides, and campfire time
- Renting a beach house to revisit your sun-soaked younger days
- A trip to a far-away friend's house for an extended slumber party, movie marathon, wine, food made by a personal chef, and at-home coziness

I'm sure your group can come up with some more ideas, and there's always that "we have to go to..." idea that you might have discussed a thousand times in the past, then no one ever had time to arrange or attend. Now's the time.

And don't forget that a girlfriends' getaway doesn't have to include any overnight stays anywhere. It can be a day trip, such as taking the train into the city to catch a show or take in a museum exhibit, a fabulous lunch or dinner at a rooftop restaurant with an amazing view of the city, or a shopping jaunt. You might go to a botanic garden for the afternoon, or on a dinner cruise, or to a day spa for everyone to get "the works" with glasses of bubbly in hand. When your group's schedules allow for just a day of quality time together, make that one day great.

Planning It Out

Okay, so how do these girls' getaways get planned with etiquette in mind? If you invite your friends on a weekend getaway, doesn't that mean you have to pay for their hotel rooms, food, and drinks? Not necessarily. (Since this is the most frequent and most pressing question about girls' getaways, I thought I'd dive right into it!) While you always have the option to treat your bridesmaids and best friends to a getaway paid for entirely by you, it's far more common for the bride and her friends to simply talk openly about the getaway with self-pay being out in the open. "Hey, ladies! I think our plan to do a girls' getaway in Chicago is do-able! I spotted a plane fare of ninety dollars and if we all stay in a three-bedroom suite, that puts each of our shares in the X-dollar range. What do you think?" Good friends can talk this openly about bill splitting without worrying about causing offense.

Also in the "make it clear and unmistakable" category, you can say, "Someday, I plan to be fabulous enough to treat each of you to an all-expenses paid getaway to Bali, but that's a few years away. ☺ How about we head off to Philly for a girls' getaway weekend, splitting the cost of a suite?" Direct and unmistakable. Your friends know what to expect. Communication is clear. That's good etiquette. And your friends can feel free to say, "Wish I could, but my budget's not going to let me take a weekend away. ☹ Maybe dinner in the city instead?" Come to a consensus, so that no friend is blocked out of the getaway due to a smaller discretionary budget. As a group, you may decide to do the day trip option instead, to everyone's budget relief. Or, as a group, you might keep researching for a less expensive getaway option.

So we've got that out of the way. Either you message your ladies with, "Wanna go on a girls' getaway trip, on me?" or you reach out with a clear message that costs will be split. Either way, the money issue is clear to all.

Next questions:

- *Who plans the girls' getaway?* It can be you, your maid or matron of honor, all of your bridesmaids, or your entire circle of friends planning it as a treat for you. I've seen grooms/partners suggest the trip, then plan and pay for it as a gift to the bride, which I think is pretty awesome. Experiences before "things," a priceless gift, especially when it gives you time with your girlfriends. (Now, don't get mad at your partner if he/she doesn't or can't plan this trip for you! There are many years down the road when this or another super-thoughtful gesture might come about.)

- *Where to stay?* You could get a discount room block at some hotels with your booking of three rooms. Call and explain that you're a bride and bridesmaids taking a getaway, and you're hoping for a room block discount rate. Hotels love to see wedding groups at their establishments, since you might love the place so much you could potentially book your wedding, bridal shower, or other event. Many hotels like to treat wedding groups like gold, such as arranging for a welcome snack spread and bottle of champagne or wine in your suite. Don't think that the number of rooms you need is too few to qualify for any special deals. It can never hurt to ask.

- *Who is invited?* You may decide to make it a bride and bridesmaids only getaway, or open your guest list up to include additional friends who— for any reason—could not be bridesmaids. Or skip the bridesmaids designation and just invite your sisters and your entire circle of close friends, whether or not they'll be bridesmaids. This is tier 1, just like your wedding guest list. If you'd like this to be a friends-only guest list allowing you more quality time with just your friends, you can draw the line here. There

Planning Tip

Consider taking over a bed-and-breakfast, so your group can chat by the fireplace as late as you'd like, stay in charming rooms with canopy beds, and gather together in the morning for a homemade breakfast. You may be surprised to find bed-and-breakfasts located just a few towns away from you . . . lovely, well-rated ones you never realized were so close by. What a great discovery for your group, who may bring out of your stay the inspiration to book a romantic getaway there with their sweethearts.

are many brides who happily extend invitations to the mothers, stepmothers, their partner's sisters and nieces for an extended circle of loved ones ready for relaxed, no-wedding-talk quality time. If you feel, though, like you'd be playing hostess between groups of guests who don't know each other well, you may wish to skip this tier 2 option. Becoming a group of thirty or forty people can make things more intense.

* *What to plan?* Make meal reservations, and get tickets for any special shows or displays you'd like to enjoy with your guests. That's about it. There's no need to plan any games or ice breakers, or decorate anything. Leave all that to the bridal shower planning team and just encourage your group to make it simple and relaxing for all, with a few planned events thrown in. Spa treatments might need to be booked months in advance, so check on that and let your guests know to log in, call, or check in with the hotel spa to arrange their own choices of treatments. Otherwise, leave your itinerary open for downtime and spontaneous outings.

* *How far in advance should you plan?* As far in advance as possible, to help ensure that all of your friends can block off room in their schedules. To make it easier, use the same time frame rules as those used for sending wedding invitations: six to eight weeks prior for a nearby event, and twelve to sixteen weeks prior for an event that will require travel planning.

* *How many days?* Most girls' getaways last a weekend, or a long weekend if you'll book for a holiday to give you extra time together. A week may be a stretch for your ladies' available time and budget, so stick to the shorter end of the scale. An overnight or day trip works well, if that works best for your group and for the location you have in mind (just an hour or two travel time to reach it).

* *What to bring?* It's a wonderful idea to bring along goodie bags for your girls, including some pampering items, spa socks, lip balms (very appreciated at winter destinations), and some wine or champagne and treats for a welcome toast.

18

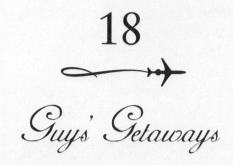

Guys' Getaways

JUST LIKE THE skipping of a racy bachelorette party can be good news for the bride (and her partner), so, too, can the skipping of the raunchy bachelor party be a good thing. Instead of club hopping and lap dances, the men can indulge in a golf resort stay, a camping trip, ski trip, or a professional sports game at a far-away stadium they've never been to—in VIP box seats.

The parameters are the same as you've just seen for the girls' getaways, with overnights or day trips helping to cut down on lofty travel expenses, and the message conveying who pays for what remains the same. Again, the groom or his best man and groomsmen may pick up the tab, or everyone can agree to split expenses.

Here are some guys' getaway styles to help inspire your groom and his circle for the planning of their own much-needed bonding escape:

- Professional sporting event at that far-away stadium or at a nearby stadium they've been to before . . . only this time upgraded to the good seats or a box

- Minor league sporting event, with box seats and all of the fun and food of a pro stadium for much less money
- Ski and snowboarding trip
- Camping trip
- A stay at a woodsy resort with adventure activities like falconry lessons and archery
- A concert, followed by a great dinner and drinks, escorted around the city in a limo
- A shore house rental for the weekend, to relive their golden beach weeks with their friends
- Dude ranch getaway, with roping, riding, and dinner by the fire
- Casino weekend
- Concert
- Food, wine, or music festival
- Seaworthy weekend, with boating and fishing
- Paintball outing
- Ironman or mudder event in a city they've never raced in
- Lake house rental, with lakeside dining and boating
- Spa resort weekend, with hiking, boot camp classes, and men's spa treatments—this is a top trend now, with many resorts tailoring their guys' getaway packages to include sauna and steam room time in addition to wraps,

Planning Tip

It is okay for the groom to choose the plan, even if the friends want to plan and pay for it. So don't be shy about sending out a link to that woodsy falconry and archery place. The guys want to plan something you'll love, and you can all work together to tailor your getaway to also include a night out drinking if that's what your guys are looking forward to.

men's manicures, and facials. Even without treatments, spa resorts are often located in amazing woodland areas with lots of activities.

- Winery or brewery tours and tastings, or a fine dinner with an expert-led Scotch tasting
- A visit to a faraway friend who can't get away. The party comes to his place, or to a hotel near him, for quality guy time.

19

Pre-Honeymoon

THIS IS A getaway just for you, a chance to unplug, unwind, and just relax in the arms of one another, recapturing that easy sense of calm that always existed between you before your wedding transformed you into someone just a bit different (or a lot different). You've missed one another while you were distracted, maybe disliked one another from time to time. But your love was always there, and now it's time to let it come back out in safety and surety. It'll just be the two of you, together.

No wedding talk.

No wedding thoughts.

No logging on to wedding blogs, Pinterest, or Instagram.

No texts from your wedding planner, boss, roommate, or anyone else who wants you to solve something or answer something. You. Are. Checked. Out. For just a few days, or perhaps for a week if this is your vacation time before your wedding next year.

This isn't your pre-visit to your wedding location, even if you'll get married in the place where you most love to vacation. It's a completely different place, a completely different mind-set.

And it's the most important pre-wedding getaway of all. This is where you reconnect with each other. And remember that, yes, you do want to spend the rest of your life with your best friend. Remembering that levels out the intensity of all of those destination wedding plans. If you're at level 5 stress over ceviche on your cocktail party menu, are you really remembering to ask your partner how his day was? Nope. Not even close.

So take the time to plan a pre-wedding getaway, and recharge your connection to each other.

- *Where to go?* Anyplace away from home, even if it's a nice hotel a few blocks away. If they have a romance package or a special weekend deal, all the better. Just the change of scenery can put you in a healthy disconnect mode from your life at home, and in a lovely room or suite, it's all about together time. Try a bed-and-breakfast for cozy style and warmth in any season, or take your show on the road to a resort a few hours away by car or plane.
- *When to go?* It's up to you. Many couples take their pre-honeymoon a month or two before the wedding, when all of the big planning steps are done. Wedding stress has accumulated, so it's a good idea to eliminate as

Budget Tip

Check out your rewards points or miles. If you have some that will expire before your wedding date, or just some extra to spare, much of your trip can be free. Which can make your getaway guilt-free as well.

much of it as possible now so that you're fresh and recharged in the weeks leading up to the wedding. New stressors may pop up then, so it's smart to flush out the old stress before it piles up too high. You may also want to take advantage of a holiday weekend or expiring vacation time whenever it occurs during your planning season.

* *How long to stay?* A weekend can give you enough time to unwind, but if you'll travel a distance a chunk of that time will be taken up by your journey on the front and back end of your getaway. If you're the type who takes a while to unwind on a vacation, aim for four or five days. And if you can do a week's vacation, all the better for ultimate relaxation, romance, dining, dancing, and true escape.

* *What to plan?* Normally, I'd say "nothing!" since your life is taken over by so much planning, but this getaway is a perfect time to plan a romantic surprise for your partner. Set up a private dinner on the beach, couple's massage, champagne and berries waiting for you in your room, and an amazing present. I also love the idea of exchanging romantic letters— just one or one for each day for your partner to find in your room, at dinner, on the beach, and so forth. If you love the love letter idea, you can either tell your partner you'll be doing this, so that he or she can do the same (not feeling left out or bad for not thinking of it!), or bring along a box of blank notecards for both of you to write out notes during the getaway.

Planning Tip

If notes aren't your style, perhaps you can exchange a little gift each day, either pre-planned or picked up at the hotel gift shop. It can be as simple as a candy bar to make a big impact.

Planning Tip

Know your wedding deadlines before you go. If you know that your bridesmaids' gown deposits are due while you're away, check in with your maid of honor before departing and ask her to send you a thumbs-up emoji while you're gone just for your peace of mind. Let your wedding planner know you're going to be away as well so that he or she can hold this time sacred for you, handling all issues for you until you get back.

• *Should it be a surprise getaway?* It can be, if your partner is the type to love surprises. I have to warn you, though, that if someone is stressed out from wedding planning, any type of surprise—even a good one—can push them over the edge. A drained person can get very upset over not knowing what to expect or not finding something they need packed for them. If you'd like to play it safe, announce the getaway in time to prepare for it. Studies show that the anticipation of a getaway leads to calming hormone production.

• *Can you set some ground rules?* You absolutely should. Set rules for no wedding talk, no family drama talk, no work talk. You might even make it a completely unplugged getaway, with no obsessive checking of social media or e-mail. It may feel strange to you both at first, difficult perhaps, and maybe impossible to disconnect entirely if you're truly hooked to your gadgets, but as much of your getaway that can be unplugged as possible, the better. Some couples with work deadlines find it better to check e-mails in the morning, respond as needed, then put their phones away. Trying to unplug completely could actually cause stress, so find the system that's right for you.

Worksheets

Destination Wedding
Countdown Calendar

10+ MONTHS

☐ Start thinking about destinations for your wedding, as a starting point to help you envision what your wedding will look and feel like.

☐ Make your priority lists to organize what's most important to you both, and which elements will get more of your budget.

☐ Research and hire your wedding planner.

☐ Decide on your wedding's size.

☐ Figure out your budget.

☐ Research and choose your wedding location and venues.

☐ Decide on your wedding date, time, and location at your venue.

☐ Research and choose your air travel flights, if needed.

☐ Research the legalities of getting married at your chosen location.

☐ Pick out your bridal party and inform them of your wedding details.

☐ Finalize your guest list.

☐ Start gown shopping.

☐ Ask your wedding coordinator to send you a list of preferred vendors, so that you can start researching and hiring them.

☐ If your wedding will be in peak season, book a hotel room block for you and for your guests.

☐ Book your pre-wedding visit to your resort or hotel for on-site wedding planning.

8–10 MONTHS

☐ Create your wedding website.

☐ Visit your wedding locations and meet with your on-site planner, vendors, and officiant to make wedding plans.

☐ Research honeymoon locations, and book your honeymoon.

☐ Continue gown shopping if you haven't yet found The One.

☐ Interview and hire your wedding vendors.

☐ Start registering for gifts.

☐ Shop with your bridesmaids for their dresses and accessories.

☐ Arrange room block and finalize details for guests.

6–8 MONTHS

☐ Send out Save the Dates.

☐ Order your gown if you haven't already.

☐ Order your veil and accessories.

☐ Finalize your bridesmaids' gown choices.

☐ Arrange for the men's wardrobe choices.

☐ Connect with your vendors about your wedding plans.

☐ Connect with your officiant about your ceremony.

☐ Research and book any wedding weekend events, such as your welcome cocktail party, dinner cruises, and activities.

☐ Get travel and wedding insurance.

☐ Check with a travel agent to see if you can book blocks of seats for your guests' airline travel.

☐ Check with your wedding location about anything that needs to be done, such as arranging for guests' ferry rides to your island wedding location, or a shuttle to the hotel.

☐ Make final decisions about your catering, cake, flowers, and other elements.

☐ Select musicians and music for your ceremony.

☐ Select and order your invitations.

☐ Select and plan with a graphic designer for your monogram or other artistic elements for your invitations.

4–6 MONTHS

☐ Confirm local marriage requirements, and start the process of handling legalities.

☐ Get or renew your passports, if needed.

☐ Send out your invitations.

☐ Select and buy your wedding rings.

3–4 MONTHS

☐ Start your wedding hair and makeup trials.

☐ Design and order your wedding programs.

☐ Check in with your wedding vendors about any needed tasks or decisions.

☐ Keep track of your RSVPs.

☐ Connect with those who wish to plan events during your wedding weekend and make arrangements.

☐ Shop for bridal party and parents' gifts, as well as gifts for each other.

☐ Update your wedding website with any new information.

☐ Check in with your coordinator for any tasks still to be done.

2 MONTHS

☐ Attend fittings for your gown.

☐ Plan any post-wedding celebration that will take place at your hometown.

☐ Get your rings engraved, if applicable.

☐ Get your rings insured.

☐ Shop for any wedding décor you'll bring with you.

☐ Plan your guests' welcome bags.

☐ Make hair and beauty appointments as needed.

☐ Attend any bridal showers thrown for you.

☐ Send thank-you notes for bridal shower gifts.

☐ Begin writing your vows.

☐ Start working on your seating chart.

☐ Shop for, buy, or make your wedding favors.

☐ Shop for any new clothes you'd like to wear during your wedding weekend.

☐ Arrange for house, pet, and plant sitters to take care of things while you're away.

☐ Create itineraries for guest welcome baskets.

☐ Make a super-detailed packing list.

☐ Review when all of your final payments are due.

3–6 WEEKS

☐ Confirm your travel reservations and check on your hotel room blocks.

☐ Finalize details with your wedding planner and vendors.

☐ Create your wedding day itinerary with your planner.

☐ Finalize your music.

☐ Ship any wedding supplies to your venue, getting tracking info and insurance.

☐ Finalize your wedding guest count.

☐ Check on legalities again, just to be sure. Find out when to apply for your marriage license and apply.

☐ Check in with your wedding planner for last-minute details and timing.

1–2 WEEKS

☐ Start packing.

☐ Send thank-you notes for any wedding gifts that arrive.

☐ Confirm your vendor meetings for when you arrive at your destination.

☐ Confirm your transportation for when you arrive at your destination.

☐ Finalize your seating plan.

☐ Create your emergency kit.

☐ Book your rides to and from the airport or dock.

☐ Make plans for your pets' boarding, if necessary.

☐ Pick up tuxedos.

THE DAY BEFORE YOU LEAVE FOR YOUR WEDDING

☐ Connect with your coordinator for any last-minute details.

☐ Connect with the bridal party to be sure they have all of their needs met.

☐ Confirm your flight.

☐ Confirm your ride to the airport or dock.

- ☐ Get cash.
- ☐ Pack, making sure you have your passports, wedding license, insurance papers, and all other important information.
- ☐ Charge your phones completely.
- ☐ Take your pets to boarding, if necessary.
- ☐ Get a good night's sleep.

UPON YOUR ARRIVAL (THIS MAY BE SEVERAL DAYS BEFORE YOUR WEDDING)

- ☐ Meet with your coordinator and vendors to review your final details.
- ☐ Give your guest welcome bags to your coordinator or hotel event manager.
- ☐ Connect with your officiant to finalize plans.
- ☐ Apply for your marriage license, if timing is right.
- ☐ Go for your trial hair and makeup session with the on-site beauty experts.
- ☐ Plan and attend a family dinner, if others will arrive early as well.
- ☐ Organize your final payments and tips.
- ☐ Plan and attend your rehearsal and rehearsal dinner.
- ☐ Relax.
- ☐ The night before, sign your marriage license.

THE DAY OF YOUR WEDDING

- ☐ Have a special breakfast with your partner or attendants.
- ☐ Have your gown steamed.
- ☐ Pose for photos.

☐ Get wedding morning massages.

☐ Get your hair, makeup, and nails done.

☐ Let your wedding planner guide you through all of the itinerary steps leading up to the wedding.

☐ Enjoy!

Wedding Guest List

Priority Lists

PRIORITY LIST 1

1. _____
2. _____
3. _____
4. _____
5. _____

PRIORITY LIST 2

1. _____
2. _____
3. _____
4. _____
5. _____

Budget

	BUDGETED	ACTUAL	NOTES
CEREMONY			
Location fee			
Transportation to ceremony location			
Officiant fee			
Officiant transportation			
Officiant lodging			
Accessories (ring pillow, candles, cultural or religious items)			
Aisle runner			
Fees for extras, like the ringing of bells			
RECEPTION			
Food for cocktail party and reception			
Bar			
Cake and cutting fees			
Desserts			
Vendor meals			
Reception venue fee			
Rentals			
Service fee or tip			

	BUDGETED	ACTUAL	NOTES
FLOWERS AND DÉCOR			
Ceremony site décor			
Reception décor			
Bride's bouquet			
Bridesmaids' bouquets			
Flower girl bouquets			
Flowers for special women guests			
Boutonnieres			
Corsages			
Flower girl wreaths			
Flowers for memorial display			
Flower petals			
Signs			
Lighting			
Rentals (tent, stage, etc.)			
Other décor			
ATTIRE			
Bride's dress			
Bride's alterations			
Veil/headpiece			
Hair accessories			
Bride's shoes			

	BUDGETED	ACTUAL	NOTES
Bride's undergarments			
2nd Look dress and accessories			
Groom's tuxedo or suit			
Groom's accessories			

BEAUTY AND SPA

	BUDGETED	ACTUAL	NOTES
Hair			
Makeup			
Spa treatments			
Tips			

RINGS AND JEWELRY

	BUDGETED	ACTUAL	NOTES
Bride's wedding band			
Groom's wedding band			
Engravings			
Bride's wedding jewelry			
Jewelry for the rehearsal dinner			

TRAVEL AND LODGING

	BUDGETED	ACTUAL	NOTES
Scouting trip			
Wedding couple travel			
Wedding couple lodging			
Meal plan			
Spending money at resort			
Limo or wedding transportation			

	BUDGETED	ACTUAL	NOTES
Guest shuttles			
Tips			

PHOTOGRAPHY AND VIDEOGRAPHY

	BUDGETED	ACTUAL	NOTES
Photographer fees			
Photo prints and enlargements			
Albums			
Images on disc			
Videographer fees			
Video editing and copies			
Photographer travel and lodging			
Videographer travel and lodging			
Assistant fees			
Video display at reception			
Photo booth rental and props			

MUSIC AND ENTERTAINMENT

	BUDGETED	ACTUAL	NOTES
Welcome party musicians			
Ceremony musicians			
Cocktail hour musicians			
Reception musicians, band or deejay			
Additional performers			
After-party musicians			

	BUDGETED	ACTUAL	NOTES
STATIONERY			
Save-the-Date cards			
Invitations			
Programs			
Place cards			
Menu cards			
Calligraphy			
Custom monogram design			
GIFTS AND FAVORS			
Guest welcome bags			
Wedding favors			
Attendants' gifts			
Parents' gifts			
Gifts to each other			
Gifts to wedding planner and other special vendors			
Other gifts			
WELCOME PARTY			
Site fee			
Catering			
Bar			
Desserts			

	BUDGETED	ACTUAL	NOTES
Décor			
Entertainment			
Tips			

WEDDING WEEKEND EVENTS

	BUDGETED	ACTUAL	NOTES
Invitations			
Site fee			
Catering			
Bar			
Desserts			
Décor			
Event tickets			
Transportation to and from event			
Spending money at event			
Special attire (T-shirts, water bottles with logo, etc.)			
Other			

REHEARSAL DINNER

	BUDGETED	ACTUAL	NOTES
Invitations			
Site fee			
Catering			
Bar			
Desserts			

	BUDGETED	ACTUAL	NOTES
Décor			
Entertainment			
AV rental (for video or slideshow)			
Tips			
AFTER-PARTY			
Invitations			
Site fee			
Catering			
Bar			
Desserts			
Décor			
Entertainment			
Special services (cigar roller, fireworks, etc.)			
Tips			
MORNING-AFTER BREAKFAST OR BRUNCH			
Invitations			
Site fee			
Catering			
Bar/drinks			
Desserts			
Décor			

	BUDGETED	ACTUAL	NOTES
Favors			
Tips			

OTHER ESSENTIALS

	BUDGETED	ACTUAL	NOTES
Wedding coordinator fee			
Wedding coordinator assistant			
Wedding coordinator travel			
Wedding coordinator lodging			
Marriage license application			
Lawyer for wills, etc.			
Wedding insurance			
Phone bill			
Data plan and overages			
Wedding website design and host-ing (if not free)			
Shipping			
Extra baggage fees			
House sitter			
Pet sitter			
Plant sitter			
Wardrobe for other events			

GIRLS' GETAWAY

	BUDGETED	ACTUAL	NOTES
Invitations			

	BUDGETED	ACTUAL	NOTES
Travel			
Lodging			
Food and drinks			
Event tickets and activity expenses			
Goodie bags or gifts			
Cash			
Tips			

GUYS' GETAWAY

	BUDGETED	ACTUAL	NOTES
Travel			
Lodging			
Food and drinks			
Event tickets and activity expenses			
Goodie bags or gifts			
Cash			
Tips			

POST-WEDDING PARTY BACK HOME

	BUDGETED	ACTUAL	NOTES
Invitations			
Site fee			
Catering			
Bar			
Cake			
Desserts			

	BUDGETED	ACTUAL	NOTES
Décor			
Entertainment			
Rentals			
Photo booth			
Photography			
Videography			
Favors			
Tips			

Contacts

Who Is Doing What?

In this section, you'll keep track of who is taking on which events and responsibilities for you.

HOSTING WEEKEND EVENTS

WELCOME COCKTAIL PARTY

Name: _____

Phone: _____

E-mail: _____

WEEKEND EVENT 1

Name: _____

Phone: _____

E-mail: _____

WEEKEND EVENT 2

Name: _____

Phone: _____

E-mail: _____

WEEKEND EVENT 3

Name: _____

Phone: _____

E-mail: _____

WEEKEND EVENT 4

Name: _____

Phone: _____

E-mail: _____

WEEKEND EVENT 5

Name: _____

Phone: _____

E-mail: _____

REHEARSAL DINNER

Name: _____

Phone: _____

E-mail: _____

AFTER-PARTY

Name: _____

Phone: _____

E-mail: _____

WEDDING MORNING BREAKFAST

Name: _____

Phone: _____

E-mail: _____

MORNING-AFTER BREAKFAST

Name: _____

Phone: _____

E-mail: _____

PARTICIPATING IN THE CEREMONY

DOING READINGS

Name: _____

Phone: _____

E-mail: _____

PERFORMING MUSIC

Name: _____

Phone: _____

E-mail: _____

OTHER

Name: _____

Phone: _____

E-mail: _____

PARTICIPATING IN THE RECEPTION

GIVING A TOAST

Name: _____

Phone: _____

E-mail: _____

INTRODUCING THE WEDDING SLIDESHOW OR VIDEO

Name: _____

Phone: _____

E-mail: _____

PERFORMING MUSIC

Name: _____

Phone: _____

E-mail: _____

OTHER

Name: _____

Phone: _____

E-mail: _____

HELP WITH PLANNING

RESEARCHING SITES AND VENDORS

Name: _____

Phone: _____

E-mail: _____

CALLING CONTACTS

Name: _____

Phone: _____

E-mail: _____

LENDING YOU WEDDING ITEMS

Name: _____

Phone: _____

E-mail: _____

DIY PROJECTS

Name: _____

Phone: _____

E-mail: _____

OTHER

Name: _____

Phone: _____

E-mail: _____

WHILE YOU'RE AWAY

PET SITTING

Name: _____

Phone: _____

E-mail: _____

PLANT SITTING

Name: _____

Phone: _____

E-mail: _____

HOUSE SITTING

    Name: _____

    Phone: _____

    E-mail: _____

GETTING PACKAGES THAT COME TO YOUR HOUSE

    Name: _____

    Phone: _____

    E-mail: _____

OTHER

    Name: _____

    Phone: _____

    E-mail: _____

OTHER

    Name: _____

    Phone: _____

    E-mail: _____

OTHER

    Name: _____

    Phone: _____

    E-mail: _____

DIY Planner

Here, you'll organize any DIY projects that you or a helpful friend or relative will make for your wedding.

PROJECTS

PROJECT 1

Description: _____

URL or site where you saw it: _____

Supplies needed: _____

Who's on the DIY team: _____

When it will be done: _____

Where it will be delivered: _____

What you'll do with it afterward (sell, lend, keep, etc.): _____

_____

PROJECT 2

Description: _____

URL or site where you saw it: _____

Supplies needed: _____

Who's on the DIY team: _____

When it will be done: _____

Where it will be delivered: _____

What you'll do with it afterward (sell, lend, keep, etc.): _____

_____

PROJECT 3

Description: _____

URL or site where you saw it: _____

Supplies needed: _____

Who's on the DIY team: _____

When it will be done: _____

Where it will be delivered: _____

What you'll do with it afterward (sell, lend, keep, etc.): _____

_____

PROJECT 4

Description: _____

URL or site where you saw it: _____

Supplies needed: _____

Who's on the DIY team: _____

When it will be done: _____

Where it will be delivered: _____

What you'll do with it afterward (sell, lend, keep, etc.): _____

_____

PROJECT 5

Description: _____

URL or site where you saw it: _____

Supplies needed: _____

Who's on the DIY team: _____

When it will be done: _____

Where it will be delivered: _____

What you'll do with it afterward (sell, lend, keep, etc.): _____

_____

Deadlines

Use this section to record any important deadlines for contract signing, deposits, details provided to vendors, and orders.

ITEM	DEADLINE DATE	✓

Ceremony Elements Wish List

Separate from your priority lists, this is where you'll list out your ideas for your ceremony. This begins as just a brainstorm, so write down anything that inspires you, and make notes on what you don't want. You'll then use this page to help as you work with your officiant to design your destination wedding ceremony. If language may be a barrier, you can also create a Pinterest board or Dropbox file of images and rituals you'd like to include for better communication.

_____

_____

_____

_____

_____

_____

_____

_____

_____

_____

_____

_____

_____

Reception Elements Wish List

And here, too, you'll list out all of the ideas you have for your reception, again starting as a brainstorm list of every idea that comes to mind, and over time fine-tuning with cross-outs and additions. This is a section that will also help you communicate with your vendors and site managers, with images helping to convey your wishes.

Food _____

_____

_____

Drinks _____

_____

Cake _____

_____

Desserts _____

_____

Décor _____

_____

_____

Entertainment _____

_____

Other _____

_____

_____

Wedding Photography Wish List

You've seen so many beautiful wedding photos during your pre-research, and you'll see plenty more as you go along. In order to convey those Must-Have shots to your photographer, and thus get all of the images you want, list out your ideas here. And again, create a Pinterest board of your favorite types of images to share with your photographer, whether or not there is a language barrier. Visuals will help your photo pro fulfill your photo wish list. And if your parents would like to participate in this process, invite them to create their own Pinterest page of photo ideas that you can share with the photographer. This is one of the easiest and most drama-free tasks for parents to participate in, and it helps ensure they get the frameable images they want, too.

_____

_____

_____

_____

_____

_____

_____

_____

_____

_____

_____

_____

_____

Wedding Weekend Event Wish List

Use this space to write down all of your ideas and wishes for the events, parties, and outings you'd like to enjoy with your destination wedding guests. This will start out as just a brainstorm, to get all of your ideas down on paper, and then you'll fine-tune it as you go. Others may offer to host certain wedding weekend events, and you might discover other ideas during your pre-wedding scouting visit. Use this list, and a Pinterest board, to work with your on-site planner and vendors if you need their work and help on any of your plans.

Welcome cocktail party _____

_____

Outings _____

_____

_____

Dinners and parties _____

_____

Sporting events _____

_____

Cocktail parties _____

_____

Rehearsal dinner _____

_____

Breakfasts _____

Other events _____

Emergency Kit

No matter where you choose to go for your destination wedding, you'll need an emergency kit to make quick work of fixing little snafus and keeping yourself comfortable throughout your wedding weekend, and especially on your wedding day. So here is a packing list of items to include in your own, custom emergency kit. You can certainly buy pre-made ones on the market—kits that include dozens of little items to help save the day—but you might want to add more or start from scratch to perfect your kit. Some items to include:

- [ ] Tissues
- [ ] Safety pins
- [ ] Fabric tape
- [ ] Mints
- [ ] Eye drops
- [ ] Extra set of contacts and solution
- [ ] Lip gloss
- [ ] Lip balm
- [ ] Sunscreen lotion, sunscreen for lips
- [ ] Lash glue
- [ ] Pressed powder
- [ ] Band-Aids—get large-size ones for the night before your wedding. The big bandages can help keep your heel straps from making painful blisters that can make shoe-wearing harder on your wedding day.
- [ ] Nail polish for touchups
- [ ] Nail polish remover pads for re-dos

- ☐ Orange stick
- ☐ Feminine products
- ☐ Emory board
- ☐ Tweezer
- ☐ Cuticle scissors
- ☐ Deodorant
- ☐ Wipes for glasses and sunglasses
- ☐ Hair bands
- ☐ Insect bite stick
- ☐ Stain stick
- ☐ Sewing kit
- ☐ EpiPen
- ☐ Inhaler
- ☐ Medicines—antacid, pain reliever, etc.
- ☐ Q-tips
- ☐ Antibacterial gel (like Purell)
- ☐ Cash/local currency—always good to have in case you need to send a guest back to the hotel in a cab, or tip a professional or worker
- ☐ Phone charger
- ☐ Adapter for your phone charger
- ☐ Other items

Bring It, Ship It, or Buy It There?

You'll need plenty of "stuff" at your wedding, and when it comes to a destination wedding, it's not always as easy as loading up a car and bringing everything you need to your wedding spot a few miles away. If your destination is overseas, on an island, on a mountain, on a cruise ship, or many hours away, you'll need a detailed plan on how to get all of your stuff there. Money will be a factor, since putting everything in a dozen suitcases is going to cost you a fortune in airline baggage fees. Shipping costs also add up. And you don't want to forget anything. So for those items that can be brought, shipped, or acquired at your wedding location, here's a chart to help your plan come together:

	BRING IT	SHIP IT	BUY IT THERE
Wedding programs			
Place cards			
Menu cards			
Family photos for display			
Cake topper			
Welcome bags			
Welcome bag contents			
Gifts for your bridal party			
Gifts for your parents			
Wedding favors			
Favors for other events			
Cake knife			
Ring bearer pillow(s)			
Flower girl basket(s)			

	BRING IT	SHIP IT	BUY IT THERE
Table runners			
Aisle runner			
Guest book and pens			
Unity candle			
Kiddush cup			
Ceremony items			
Reception décor items			
1.			
2.			
3.			
4.			
5.			
6.			
7.			
8.			
9.			
10.			
Wedding weekend items (printed T-shirts, cups, etc.)			
Something old			
Something new			
Something borrowed			
Something blue			

	BRING IT	SHIP IT	BUY IT THERE
Electrical converters/adapters			
CDs/music			
Other items			

GIRLS' TURN

Guest list: _____

_____

_____

_____

_____

_____

Location ideas: _____

_____

_____

_____

_____

Location inquiries: _____

_____

_____

_____

_____

_____

Location chosen: _____

_____

_____

_____

_____

_____

Events and details: _____

_____

_____

_____

_____

_____

Vendor contacts: _____

_____

_____

_____

_____

_____

GUYS' TURN

Guest list: _____

_____

_____

_____

_____

Location ideas: _____

_____

_____

_____

_____

Location inquiries: _____

_____

_____

_____

_____

_____

Location chosen: _____

_____

_____

_____

_____

_____

Events and details: _____

_____

_____

_____

_____

Vendor contacts: _____

_____

_____

_____

_____

Resources

Here are some websites that may be of use to you while you're planning your wedding and all of your getaway events.

We provide these resources and others throughout the book merely as a guide, and encourage you to use your best diligence in checking them out before shopping there, hiring a professional from the site, or engaging with any of their advertisers. These sites are not endorsed by me, nor by the publisher. So shop at your own discretion.

Beauty

Avon.com

BobbiBrown.com

CareFair.com

Clinique.com

ElizabethArden.com

EsteeLauder.com

Eve.com

iBeauty.com

Lancome.com

L'oreal.com

MacCosmetics.com

MakeoverStudio.com

MaxFactor.com

Maybelline.com

Neutrogena.com

Pantene.com

Revlon.com

Sephora.com

YouTube.com

Hairstyles

About.com

Beauty-and-the-Bath.com

DIY-Weddings.com

eHow.com

HairstyleZone.com

HerbalEssences.com

Suave.com

UpDoPrincess.com

VideoHairstyles.com

YouTube.com

Wedding Planning Websites

100LayerCake.com

BridalGuide.com

Brides.com

DestinationIDoMag.com

GetMarried.com

GreenWeddingShoes.com

Idoforbrides.com

MarthaStewart.com

MunaluchiBride.com

PolkaDotBride.com

SouthernBride.com

StyleMePretty.com

TheKnot.com

TownandCountry.com

WeddingChannel.com

WellWed.com

Invitations

AnnaGriffin.com

BotanicalPaperworks.com

CeciNewYork.com

Crane.com

Evite.com

Hallmark.com

InviteSite.com

MomentalDesigns.com

MountainCow.com

PaperStyle.com

Papyrus.com

Preciouscollection.com

PSAEssentials.com

WeddingPaperDivas.com

Quotes and Poetry

QuoteGarden.com

QuotesandSayings.org

QuotesPlanet.com

@TheLoveStories

Music and Lyrics

iTunes.com

LyricsDepot.com

LyricsFreak.com

Romantic-Lyrics.com

Spotify.com

Flowers and Greenery

About.com
BHG.com
FloralDesignInstitute.com
HGTV.com
PAllenSmith.com
RomanticFlowers.com
SierraFlowerFinder.com

Crafts and Paper

BHG.com
FlaxArt.com
HobbyLobby.com
MarthaStewart.com
Michaels.com
OfficeMax.com
PaperDirect.com
Scrapjazz.com
Staples.com

Travel

Bed-and-Breakfast Finder:
    Bnbfinder.com
Driving Directions: Google Maps at
    maps.google.com
Tourism Offices Worldwide:
    360travelguide.com/tourist.asp
    and State.gov

Weather: Weather.com

Price Comparison Sites

@AboutFreebies
BizRate.com
Dealtime.com
NextTag.com
PriceGrabber.com
Shopping.com
Shopzilla.com

Coupon Sources

AllYou.com
CouponCabin.com
CouponDivas.com
CouponMom.com
Coupons.com
Groupon.com
RetailMeNot.com
SwagGrabber.com

Bridal Expos

BridalShowcase.com
BridalShowExpo.com
Brideworld.com
ElegantBridalProductions.com
GreatBridalExpo.com

HereComestheGuide.com
TheBlingEvent.com
TheWeddingSalon.com
WeddingWire.com/bridalshows

Additional Sites of Interest

Hangouts.Google.com—Free video chatting for up to ten people

JetFeteblog.com—Destination wedding blog

Postable.com—Gather all of your guests' addresses on this secure site to send to your stationer, calligrapher, and wedding planner

TheManRegistry.com—Info grooms and groomsmen will love

TheStylishDresser.com—Your style concierge

WeddingMapper—Create your own wedding map, share the URL, and use their seating tool and budget tracker for free

WeddingWire.com—For reviews and contact information for venues and vendors

WilliamsSonoma.com—Free cooking classes and events

Acknowledgments

My thanks to Michaela Hamilton, my stellar editor at Kensington Books, and my equally stellar agent Meredith Bernstein, as well as to my assistant Kayla Langborgh, Joseph Toris, Jenny Orsini of Jenny Orsini Events, Lisa Plociniak of A Touch of Elegance Events, Camille Cerria of Smooth Sailing Celebrations, Krystina Kennedy of Congress Hall in Cape May, NJ, Pete Malone of 217 Photography, Sage Hammond of Crown Images, Debbie Ryan of Deborah Ann Photography, Jackie Averill of Jackie Averill Photography, Kristin Rockhill of Details of I Do, and Danielle Richards of Danielle Richards Photography, among others whose professionalism and keen eye for detail added much to this book. I am so grateful to know these excellent pros.

Index